EFFECTIVE CAR DEALER

MAX ZANAN

TABLE OF CONTENTS

PREFACE. vii

1 LEADERSHIP 1

2 SALES (NEW AND USED) 3

    Program Knowledge. 5

    Phone and Email Skills 6

    Transactional Website 7

    Remote Work 10

    Merchandising. 12

    Out Of State Registration And Title. 15

    Vehicle Return/Exchange 16

    Customer Retention 17

        Centralized System. 18

    Advertising 19

    One Price 22

    Compensation Plans 24

    Training 25

3 FINANCE DEPARTMENT 26
   Hiring the Right Finance Managers 28
   Qualifications 30
   Realistic Profit Expectations and Compensation Plans . 33
   Selecting the Right F&I Vendor 36
   Selecting the Right Mix of F&I Products 38
   Preload Programs 40
       The Value of Preinstalled Add-Ons 40
       The Importance of Up-Selling 41
       Draw Attention to the Add-Ons 41
   Dealer-Branded Prepaid Maintenance 43
   Reinsurance of F&I Products 45
   Working with The Service Department 47
   Displaying F&I Products Online 48
       The F&I Department 48
       How Do We Change F&I for the Digital World? . . 49
       Don't Keep It A Secret 49
   Understanding Proper Workload 50
   Menu Presentation 51
   Unsold Customer Follow-Up 53
   Smooth Cancellation Process 54
   F&I Takeaways 55

4 F&I COMPLIANCE 56
   Safeguards Rule 60
   Red Flags Rule 66
       Elements of Red Flags Rule 67
   First: Identify Relevant Red Flags 68
   Second: Detect Red Flags 71
       New Accounts 71
       Note Suspicious Behavior 71
   Third: Prevent And Mitigate Identity Theft 72
   Fourth, Update The Program 73
   Administering Dealership Red Flags Program 74
   OFAC 75

OFAC Compliance 75
Best Practice Tip 76
Record Retention. 76
OFAC Penalties. 77
Privacy Rule 78
Compliance. 80
Form 8300 86
Type of Payments to Report 86
What Does Cash Include? 87
Definition of a Related Transaction. 87
Required Written Statement for Customers. 88
Reporting Suspicious Transactions 88
When to Report Payments 89
Multiple Payments. 89
Recordkeeping. 90
Taxpayer Identification Number (TIN). 90
Civil Penalties 90
Criminal Penalties 90
Truth In Lending Act. 91
Truth in Lending Act 91
Consumer Leasing Act 91
TILA Disclosures. 92
CLA Disclosures 92
Truth in Lending and Consumer Leasing
Act Penalties 94
Fair Credit Compliance Program 95
Uniform F&I Product Pricing 98
Risk-Based Pricing. 99
Adverse Action Notice. 100
Zero Tolerance Policies 101
Falsifying credit applications 101
Power booking used cars. 101
Payment packing and jamming F&I products. . . . 101
Consequences for the Dealer Principal 102
Two Reasons For A Robust Compliance Program 104

5 SERVICE 105
    Importance of Service and Parts 107
    Service Department Advertising 108
        Top 8 Most Common Vehicle Repairs 109
    Service Advisor Workload and Training 111
    Using Technology in the Service Department 116
    Critical KPIs to Monitor in Service 117
        Production Capacity 117
        Hours Sold Per Repair Order 118
        Effective Labor Rate 119
        Shop Policy Expense 119
        Warranty Compliance 120
        Service Absorption 120
    Increasing Effective Labor Rate 121
    Pickup And Home Delivery 123
    Shop Safety 124

6 PARTS 126
    Answering the Phone 128
    Buying Parts 130
    Parts Gross Profit 131
    Wholesale Parts Sales 132
    Selling Parts Online 133
    Selling Accessories 135
    Parts Obsolescence 137
    Quick Lube And Upselling 138
    Parts Level Of Service 139
    Days' Supply 140
    Emergency Purchases 141
    Perpetual Parts Inventory 142
    DMS Settings and Tech Proficiency 143

CONCLUSION 145

PREFACE

My name is Max Zanan and I love the car business! I've been in this business for 20 years and hope to be in it for 20 more. My goal is to do whatever it takes to help car dealers improve operations. I have written three books on the subject – *Perfect Dealership: Surviving The Digital Disruption, Car Business 101: #CrazyShitCarDealersDo*, and *The Art and Science of Running a Car Dealership*—and then COVID-19 happened and changed everything!

I wrote this book during the COVID-19 lockdown because this crisis gave me an opportunity to really think through the variable and fixed operations of the car business and how they need to change. Working on this book helped me keep my sanity and maintain a schedule. More importantly, I want to do my part to help rebuild automotive retail, post coronavirus.

I have been fortunate to have grown up in the car business and to have worked in every department of a car dealership. I started as salesperson, and over the years I've worked as a sales manager, finance manager, general sales manager, service manager, and general manager. By the age of 29, I ran the #1 Mitsubishi dealership in the country in both volume and profit. I ended my automotive retail career running an auto group that broke multiple sales and gross profit records.

I moved on to providing income development services through Finance &Inisurance(F&I) products and training, and later opened Total Dealer Compliance—one of the best dealership compliance firms in the country.

In addition to F&I and Compliance, I provide dealership consulting services that are focused on process improvement, customer retention, and profitability.

My experience uniquely qualifies me to write this book because I know the business and see it from all angles.

The problem that we have is that there is very little professional training available. There is no car sales management major at a local university, and very few dealer principals graduated from the NADA Academy or sent their general managers there.

This book is designed for general managers, aspiring general managers, dealer principals, their children, as well as dealership investors. We will cover the following topics:

- Leadership

- Sales Process

- F&I Process

- F&I Compliance

- Parts and Service

- Advertising (both customer acquisition and customer retention)

In addition, we will review real-world tools such as software, products, and service solutions that will help you take your dealership to the next level.

Ladies and Gentlemen, start your engines and let's get rolling!

1
LEADERSHIP

BEFORE WE GET into technical details, let's talk about leadership and what it means for the success of your dealership. The definition of leadership is the action of leading a group of people or an organization. The key word is *action*. Just because you have the title doesn't make you a leader. True leaders create a mission statement and a set of corporate values, an action plan to achieve your mission, and an organizational culture that allows employees to thrive.

Why do you need a mission statement? Because without it, you don't know where you are going.

Why do you need corporate values? Because if you don't stand for something, you will fall for anything.

Why do you need an action plan? Because without a plan, all you have is a dream.

Why do you need organizational culture? Because you have to inspire people to be a part of the team. Happy employees always mean happy customers.

I can't tell you what to do here—each leader must figure out on his own all of the elements above. That's the art of running a car dealership. The rest is science.

One last note on leadership—creating a healthy organizational culture together with fair pay, normal hours, training, and opportunity for career growth will drastically decrease employee turnover and increase customer satisfaction and gross profit. The opposite is also true!

There are many good books on leadership, and I recommend you take the time to read on this topic. My favorite books are:

- *Extreme Ownership. How US Navy Seals Lead and Win* by Jocko Willink and Leif Babib

- *Delivering Happiness* by Tony Hsieh

- *Uncontainable: How Passion, Commitment, and Conscious Capitalism Built a Business Where Everyone Thrives* by Kip Tindell

2
SALES (NEW AND USED)

YOUR VISION AND mission statement will drive the way in which you sell cars. Do you want to be a high-volume (for example, #1 in your zone, district, country), lowest-price dealer? Or do you just want to do a good job and let chips fall where they may. There is no right answer.

Below are the basics that you will need to master:

- Product knowledge
- Program knowledge
- Phone skills
- Email skills
- Transactional website
- Remote work

3

- Merchandising
- Vehicle return/exchange
- Out of state registration and title
- Customer retention
- Advertising
- One Price
- Pay Plans
- Training

PRODUCT KNOWLEDGE

This is straightforward. The salesperson should know the vehicles inside out and should be tested for this knowledge. Under no circumstances do you want the customer thinking she knows more about the vehicle than the salesperson. Knowing everything there is to know about a car and its features will help regain some of the lost control in the sales transaction. Again, product knowledge among your staff must be tested. Walk-around competitions are a great way to learn the product, as it motivates sales staff with prizes.

Don't keep product knowledge a secret—let your customers know that you have the most knowledgeable staff. Record walk-arounds and proudly display them on your YouTube channel.

Salespeople should also be able to record a walk-around and email it to the customer. Make sure the video is incorporated into your sales process. No fancy equipment needed— a smartphone will do. This approach is much better than sending a generic message.

Program Knowledge

Cars are becoming more and more expensive every year, and most consumers cannot afford to pay cash. The majority either finance or lease. Your sales team must know all available programs (special rates, money factors, rebates, etc.) in order to structure the deal properly so that the customer gets the best deal possible. Sometimes certain trim levels or models have more favorable programs, and customers must be made aware of these options. It is important that your finance department clearly communicates with the sales department regarding current programs and incentives.

Phone and Email Skills

There is a certain phone and email etiquette when it comes to business calls and emails. It is your responsibility to teach it to your employees. You can't assume that your staff is capable of writing a professional email or making a professional call. Part of employee onboarding should be a class on proper business communications. There are tools available to address this issue; for example, www.grammarly.com. Grammarly makes sure that everything you type is effective and error-free.

When it comes to phone skills, it is important to have basic scripts that make your staff sound professional. Using a BDC training company makes a huge difference.

Vendors

One such company is **Phone Ninjas. www.phoneninjas.com**

BDC training is all they do. One of my favorite products is Mystery Shopping, and I highly recommend it if you are serious about having a finger on the pulse of your dealership.

Transactional Website

Digital retail is real and here to stay. I bet you buy stuff from Amazon, Walmart, as well as other retailers all the time. The car business is no different, and companies such as Carvana and Vroom have proved the concept that consumers are willing to buy vehicles online. Carvana sold 177,549 cars in 2019!

COVID-19 put everything in perspective in terms of digital retail. If your dealership wasn't set up to sell cars online, in many cases you were literally out of business because customers weren't allowed to come to the showroom.

Amazon, Carvana, and Uber retrained all of us when it comes to shopping. We expect transparency and convenience. If your dealership doesn't display vehicle prices and F&I products, or provide a firm offer for a trade-in, then you are missing the boat and losing market share.

Vehicle prices, lease payments, F&I products and their respective prices are not top-secret and customers **should not** have to fill out any form to obtain this information. Transparency doesn't mean you make less money; frankly, it means the opposite.

Here is a perfect example: when menus first came out, dealers and finance managers were panicking, thinking that the world had come to an end. Nowadays, using a menu is a standard operating procedure, and dealers are averaging record-breaking numbers in the back.

It could be that COVID-19 is going to change consumer behavior, and fewer people will be willing to come to the dealership to buy a car. If that ends up being the case, you should consider a total reorganization and redesign of your sales process. Before the pandemic, your Business Development Center (BDC) was strictly selling appointments, and this approach might not be as effective now.

The key is to **redesign your BDC**. BDC must sell cars now!

This means that all salespeople, sales managers, and finance managers are effectively BDC employees. You have to empower them to sell cars over the phone, via email or text messaging, or using video conferencing. They have to be able to structure deals and conduct F&I presentations remotely.

Don't assume that your employees know how to use these tools, such as video conferencing. It is your responsibility to teach them. Again, just look at Carvana or Vroom—they are just transactional websites with a heavy-duty BDC department.

Transactional websites will help you sell cars outside of your market, and that's great news! Make sure that you know what it takes and how much it costs to ship the car to the customer in another state. Make sure you have a shipping calculator on your website.

There are good tools available out there and you will find them in the vendor section below. Regardless of the tool you choose, please make sure that you mystery shop your own website to understand what your customers are experiencing. Is it easy to use? Is it intuitive? And so on.

Vendors

Roadster. www.roadster.com
Their solution allows the customer to do the following:

1. Easily find the perfect car.

2. Get pricing info upfront.

3. Build a deal in minutes.

4. Value a trade-in.

5. Add service and protection plans.

6. Accessorize.

7. Finalize the deal.

8. Schedule pickup or delivery.

AutoFi. www.autofi.com

AutoFi's digital retail solution converts shoppers to buyers with interactivity to:

- Select a car conveniently from a mobile device or in-store.

- Evaluate price.

- Structure the deal.

- Value trade-ins.

- Add protection plans.

Data-enhanced leads ensure that Sales is in control every step of the way, communicating by email, phone, or text. With full-spectrum lender integration and real-time lender decisions, this is a fast, convenient, and transparent way of improving retention, customer satisfaction, and profitability.

ShipYourCarNow.com

ShipYourCarNow provides easy and stress-free shipping services:

- Ship Your Car Now is a Consumer Affairs accredited company.

- Fully licensed Ocean Transport Intermediary, Domestic Freight Forwarder, and Property Broker.

- $250,000 Contingent Cargo Insurance, in addition to the cargo insurance each carrier has in place.

- 24/7/365 Dispatch/Customer service department

- Vehicle Shipping – big and small, we ship them all! (Boats too).

Remote Work

I never thought that remote work and car sales could be used in the same sentence. Then Carvana came along and proved that cars could be sold remotely. Unfortunately, most dealers didn't pay attention and completely dismissed Carvana. Then COVID-19 put everything in perspective. It doesn't matter if you believe in digital retail and home delivery. What matters is that your customers believe in it, so you either adopt it or file for bankruptcy.

Many states have allowed remote sales during the COVID-19 pandemic, and that means your salespeople and finance managers had to work from home. I know a few dealers that quickly figured out how to sell cars remotely.

Now that lockdown restrictions are being loosened up, car dealers want their staff to come back to the showroom. I believe that this is extremely shortsighted. Remote work is possible and improves the quality of life of salespeople and finance managers. Remote work is possible as long as your people know how to use Customer Relationship Mananagement (CRM), Dealership Mananagement System (DMS), video conferencing and Dealertrack/RouteOne. Allowing remote work will improve the quality of your workforce because you will be able to hire people from all over the country.

My advice is not to jump the gun and dismiss remote sales as if the COVID-19 pandemic never happened. Instead, incorporate it into your sales process. Ultimately you need to perfect remote sales process because there is a possibility of additional lockdowns in case of the 2nd or 3rd wave.

Vendors

Dealer Socket/Automate. www.dealersocket.com
Dealer Socket offers a suite of powerful products:

- CRM

- DMS

- Inventory Management

- Equity Mining

- Websites and Digital Marketing

MAX Digital. www.maxdigital.com

MAX Digital is known in the inventory world for their FirstLook suite, which pioneered retail performance analytics. Today they offer a much broader set of products that cover the full retail process, from acquiring the cars most likely to sell in your dealership to providing the omnichannel experiences to sell them. What is unique about their approach is the level of consumer research and partnership. They will typically go deep into the process with one or two large groups, with a focus to significantly outperform available options. Products aren't launched until they are proven in the market.

From better managing vehicle-content accuracy with MAX Ad and MAX Digital Showroom to MAX My Trade, which naturally drives lower valuation through guided customer collaboration, each product is road tested against competitive solutions to deliver a superior return. Early products are not as attractive as their current innovations, but all leverage a solid data platform, and they continue to set the standard in the business and achieve their mission to deliver proven results.

Merchandising

Merchandising is the activity of promoting the sale of goods, especially by their presentation in retail outlets. Unfortunately, I see that many dealers completely ignore this valuable tool.

Sam Walton, the founder of Walmart, was an amazing merchandiser, and taking full advantage of merchandising allowed Walmart to outsell Sears and K-Mart.

Effective merchandising will help you sell more cars, F&I products, and parts & labor. Let's start with car sales. First impressions matter, and your frontline is that first impression. Vehicle display ramps and side-tilt displays make a huge difference. Keep in mind that merchandising is not just for the cars outside. Rock displays look amazing in the showroom. In addition, accessorizing vehicles in the showroom will increase your accessories sales. Displaying bent rims in the F&I office will help you sell more tire and wheel policies. Displaying dirty cabin filters and worn brakes will generate additional business for your parts and service departments.

Let's not forget your virtual frontline—your website. Make sure that you have multiple pictures of each vehicle for sale. For example, both Carvana and Vroom display over 20 pictures of each vehicle in stock. Another key point—do not use stock photos; your customers want to see the actual car. Have a system for taking photos. All cars must be photographed from the same angles. I would encourage you to use a photobooth to standardize and speed up the photo-taking process.

Finally, most dealers miss out on the opportunity to merchandise the dealership itself. Why not give each customer who buys a car a dealer-branded tote bag containing a t-shirt, baseball hat, umbrella, coffee mug, etc.? These items are not expensive, and your customers will proudly use them, thereby promoting your store.

Vendors

360Booth www.360booth.com

Don't be fooled into thinking that your customers would like fake backgrounds. Build a real brand at your store by showing your customers that your store will go to great lengths to provide useful photos of the actual cars, shot in a showroom studio-like setting. Fake backgrounds on your photos will only do and say one thing: you're hiding something. Don't hide behind fake backgrounds.

360Booth has the hottest and simplest studio quality auto photo booth solution available for automotive dealers. Not only will this solution give you the professional looking photos you have been looking for, but every photo will have your dealer's logo, corporate brand and identity.

Automotive Professional Displays www.vehicledisplays.com

We at Automotive Promotional Products have been designing and manufacturing Vehicle Display Platforms since early 1980. We have been in the automotive field since 1965 dealing with parts and service. Then in 1980, we became involved in vehicle displays offered to car dealerships, auto enthusiasts, and car shows promoters. They have been so effective that we do a tremendous amount of repeat business.

We ship our products worldwide and have thousands of customers around the world. We have customers in every state and over 20 countries around the world.

Not only do we make the models shown, but custom units to fit your own needs and usage.

It will be your best 24/7 marketing tool.

Dealership-Branded Merchandise
www.4imprint.com

These guys can produce anything with your dealership logo on it.

- Bags
- Mugs
- Pens
- Stationery
- Apparel
- Toys, and so much more

Out Of State Registration And Title

If you are serious about digital retail, you need to:

- Have a transactional website

- Know how to ship cars

- Know how to register cars in all 50 states

Most likely, your DMV clerks know how to handle registration and title in nearby states. For example, if your dealership is located in New York, your staff knows how to register a car in New Jersey and Florida, but I doubt that they know how to register and title a car in Montana, New Mexico, or Alaska. The following website helps you overcome this obstacle.

Vendors

50 State DMV. www.50statedmv.com
Commercial title and registration processing for all 50 states. Fastest turnaround time in the industry.

Vehicle Return/Exchange

In the not so distant past, it was unthinkable for a dealership to take a car back. The standard line was, "Is this your signature? Then enjoy your car!" In other words, go pound sand.

This approach is not going to work in today's environment. Carvana built their marketing campaign around the fact that they offer a seven-day, no-questions-asked return policy.

If you are serious about earning consumers' trust and being competitive with online retailers, then you have to offer some form of vehicle return/exchange policy. It doesn't have to be 7 days, but I want to encourage you to offer at least a 3-day exchange policy. Your goal is to remove friction from the buying process.

The vast majority of customers have no intention of returning or exchanging a car unless they have a really good reason. Being on the customer's side during these rare occurrences will buy you an incredible amount of goodwill.

In addition, I suggest you incorporate your return/exchange policy into your marketing and advertising campaigns.

Customer Retention

Most car dealers spend enormous amounts of money on attracting new customers. It is not unheard of to spend between $700-$900 per unit sold in certain areas of the country and certain franchises.

Here is some breaking news. It is significantly cheaper—as much as seven times cheaper—to retain a customer than to acquire a new one. So what can you do to accomplish that?

First and foremost, it is not enough to just sell a car anymore. You must sell the dealership and the experience that your dealership provides throughout the ownership period.

For example, what does your loyalty program look like? Do you even have one? Every supermarket, airline, and gas station has a loyalty program; your dealership should have one too!

Once the car is sold, it is mission-critical to have the customer come back to your facility for maintenance and repair. I am a big fan of Engine for Life and Dealer-Owned Pre-Paid Maintenance programs. Equity mining is another great tool that will help you sell more cars.

Besides service retention, dealerships need to communicate with sold customers on a regular basis. Let your customers know if there are new car clinics, specials on accessories, referral fees, etc.

Never forget the lifetime value of each customer. Once you understand this concept, you will stop focusing on just selling cars and start focusing on earning that each customer's business year after year.

Vendors

Dealership for Life. www.dealershipforlife.com

Dealership for Life was started in 2004 to help dealers achieve superior customer retention in their marketplace. Dealership for Life is the number one provider of why-buy-here, why-service-here programs in the United States. Blending multiple lifetime programs with proprietary software, they have created a seamless administration process that achieves state-of-the-art results.

A creative blend of individualized customer websites, customer-centric apps, digital marketing, and a world-class rewards program allows the dealer to have real-time interaction with everyone in their database on a daily basis. Customer loyalty is the Holy Grail of any business, and no one does it better than Dealership for Life.

Dealer Maintenance. www.dealermtc.com

Build a customized loyalty program to increase your customer retention rate from 20%-30% to 60%-80%. It's important that you increase your chances of selling your customers their next vehicle.

Centralized System

Our web-based system simplifies contract and claim management and provides valuable data to grow your business.

Support & Training

> We provide onsite training for your sales team and ongoing support to ensure you have everything you need to promote, sell, and fulfill your PPM & Loyalty program.

Increased Profit

> Watch your service department revenue grow and thrive. Get paid to service your customers better than ever before.

Advertising

I am not going to tell you how to advertise. Advertising is a true art, and different approaches are more effective for certain makes and geographies.

However, the goal of any advertising campaign is to ensure that the dealership stands out from the competition. It is up to you to create the message, and then your advertising company will put bells and whistles on it.

If you don't have a good message, if you offer no added value, you will have no choice but to compete on price. And we all know that competing on price is just a race to the bottom and doesn't produce customer loyalty.

Here are some examples of advertising campaigns for you to consider:

- Buy Online
- Home Delivery
- Return/Exchange Policy
- Loyalty Program
- Service Pick-Up and Delivery
- Sanitized Cars
- Referral Fee
- Local Community Involvement

Now let's talk about where to advertise. Even though the internet is where most consumers do their research, it doesn't mean that you have to ignore direct mail, radio, and TV. Also, pay attention to streaming services such as Netflix and Hulu. At some point, they will start selling advertising, and their platforms must be a part of your advertising campaign.

Vendors

The Ram Group. www.theramgroup.com

The RAM Group is a high-touch, highly consultative automotive marketing agency that specializes in both digital and traditional advertising. We use a data-driven approach to deliver effective strategies that yield both exceptional and measurable results through both digital and traditional forms. We were one of the first agencies to bring these two forms of advertising together for symbiotic marketing, managed under one roof, and with one point of contact. We are a strategic consulting partner with an ROI focus that provides the most advanced marketing solutions for our clients, ensuring their profitability with full transparency. With a multitude of ways to engage with consumers, we ensure our teams are being continually educated and trained to be subject matter experts. This gives us the ability to execute at a much higher level than others. There is nothing about us that is cookie-cutter. We provide solutions that are fully tailored to you and your business. We will never call you Monday morning and say, "What do you want to do this week?"

Premium Productions. www.premium123.com

Since 1997, Premium Productions, Inc. has been a factory-direct source for producing complete **direct-mail campaigns** from start to finish. We also develop highly responsive **email campaigns** that can be integrated with your mail campaigns, which generate increased traffic to your website and greater awareness of your offers, providing you quality leads and more sales. We have built our reputation on escalating results with a team of very qualified individuals experienced in recognizing the market trends to improve your marketing success.

As a full-service marketing company, our goal is to help you achieve your marketing objectives by encompassing market research and analytics, custom-designed creative, data sourcing, as well as production and fulfillment, to ensure you maximize the return on your investment.

For over 20 years, we have created dynamic, innovative and targeted marketing campaigns which have consistently yielded positive results. These campaigns work as an essential part of your marketing plan, matching your offers to the most targeted prospects. The production happens in-house at our production facility in Phillipsburg N.J. which ensures rapid turnaround at the best value.

One Price

One Price is something that customers understand instinctively. Every online retailer is one price, whether it is Bloomingdales, Amazon, Macy's. Don't let anyone tell you that customers like coming to the showroom to haggle—that's fake news of the highest order. Carvana and CarMax sold close to 1 million cars in 2019, both organizations are One Price, and both organizations maintain a healthy profit per-unit-retailed. For example, Carvana is hovering around $3000 gross profit per car. Customers will pay a premium for transparency and convenience.

Moreover, if you are serious about digital retail, you absolutely must be a One Price dealership. How else will you be able to sell cars online? What is the customer supposed to put in the shopping cart?

More importantly, if customers have to call you to find out the price or fill out a form to Unlock the E-Price, you are in denial and refusing to face reality. If you don't display the price of the car, your customers are moving on to the next website. It is that simple.

Remember that if your value proposition resonates with customers, they will pay a premium for it. If you got nothing to bring to the table, then you will have no choice but to compete on price and eventually be out of business.

One Price is not just about digital retail, it is about traditional showroom sales as well. I bought a car from a One Price dealership, and it was one of the best buying experiences. The price was displayed on each vehicle, and I never had anxiety about overpaying or being taken advantage of. The salesperson didn't have to sell me the price, the payment, or the interest rate. The salesperson explained what made that car special and how it compared to competition in terms of equipment and fuel economy. The salesperson had in-depth product knowledge, and the entire process was smooth and easy.

Switching to One Price is not easy and requires a major commitment from the senior management. One Price is not something you try for one day or one week. You go all-in for good! You will need to overhaul your dealership culture, your marketing, advertising, training, and compensation plans.

Switching to One Price is hard, but it is the future; and if you are serious about surviving, then you will have no choice but to do it.

Compensation Plans

Compensation is another form of art. There is no secret sauce or formula; you will need to figure out what works best for each position.

As more and more millennials enter the workforce, the more adjustments old-school car dealers will have to make. Younger people are not as motivated by money or higher commissions, the way baby boomers and generation Z were. They are also more interested in quality of life, so you might as well forget about bell-to-bell hours.

Base salary and a volume bonus will do the trick, especially if you are a One Price dealership. That volume bonus doesn't even have to be paid in American dollars. Millennials are motivated by experiences, so a trip to a Caribbean island or the OEM's racetrack might be more effective.

It is a good idea to have additional targets that salespeople must hit in order to make more money. CSI, number of referrals, completed training, and dress code are just a few ideas for you to consider.

Training

"What if I train them and they leave?" My answer is, "What if you don't and they stay?"

There is a variety of training that must be available to your employees. We've discussed product knowledge, phone, and email skills training previously. Below are some additional ideas for training:

- Customer Service

- Leadership

- Merchandising

- Online Advertising

- Ethics and Compliance

Your senior management team must encourage employees to go through as much training as possible because everyone will win. The key is to train **everybody**. Your receptionist and cashier need training as much as your salespeople. Customer service and phone skills must be mandatory for all employees.

3
FINANCE DEPARTMENT

IN THIS CHAPTER, we will cover the Finance Department and what it takes to set up a great one. Here is my definition of a great finance department:

> The finance department is an integral part of a car dealership, employing professionals who are tasked with obtaining financing and generating profits through the sale of service contracts, ancillary products, and marking up interest rates.

In addition, a finance department works closely with sales and service department towards a common goal of customer satisfaction and retention.

Let's dissect this definition.

First, what is F&I? F&I stands for Finance and Insurance. It is mostly Finance now, because car dealers stopped selling Credit Life and Credit Disability Insurance a long time ago.

Second, what does it do? F&I is tasked with obtaining financing and generating profits through the sale of service contracts, ancillary products, and marking up interest rates.

Third, the finance department is not a standalone entity; it is an integral part of the overall dealership's operation. It must work closely with sales and service department to ensure customer satisfaction and retention.

What are the risks of an improperly run Finance Department? A tremendous amount of liability in terms of fines, penalties, and reputational damage.

We will review the following topics:

1. Hiring the right finance managers.

2. Establishing realistic profit expectations and pay plans.

3. Selecting the right F&I vendor.

4. Selecting the right mix of F&I products.

5. Reinsurance and dealer-branded pre-paid maintenance.

6. Displaying F&I products on the dealership's website.

7. Understanding the proper workload.

8. Menu presentation.

9. Unsold customer follow-up.

Hiring the Right Finance Managers

Let's start with hiring the right finance managers. As you know, talented, customer-focused personnel are the key to success in any business. The following quote is one of the founding principles of The Container Store, one of the most respected and profitable retailers in the country.

> "One great person equals three good people. This is our hiring philosophy. Talent is the whole ball game. We're wild-eyed fanatics when it comes to hiring great people. We're constantly on the lookout for amazing employees who elevate the game of everyone around them to a new level."

If you put The Container Store quote in perspective, it means that one great finance manager will be as productive as three good finance managers. And therefore, you should be able to pay them more than the industry average. Just imagine the level of talent your dealership can attract if you pay 30%, 50%, or even 100% more than the competition.

Here is another quote from Kip Tindell, the founder of The Container Store:

> "Another important aspect of our 1=3 philosophy: Since we're getting at least three times the productivity from our employees (it's a purposeful understatement – you can actually get much, much more than three times the productivity at certain endeavors), we can afford to pay the people closest to the customer – our salespeople – 50 to 100 percent higher than the retail average, to communicate with them breathlessly, and to provide excellent benefits, hundreds of hours of training, and a happy place to go to work every day."

It's a win-win-win.

✓ The employee wins because she's getting paid twice as much and gets to work alongside other great people.

✓ The company wins because it's getting three times the productivity at two times the payroll cost.

✓ And our customers win because they're getting great service from highly-motivated employees.

This philosophy is really hard for car dealers to process. Once you grasp it, though, I promise you will see magic happening in your F&I department.

Qualifications

So what qualifications should you be looking for when hiring finance managers?

Let's start with the basics—criminal background checks. Make sure you do them. There is no need to hire people with felonies and misdemeanors. There are plenty of talented people out there. If you can't find them, then promote from within. People that you promote from within will be much more loyal to you and your organization in the long run.

Now let's take it a step further and consider credit checks. Credit history is a pretty good reflection of character, and plenty of employees use it to make hiring decisions. Also, insurance companies use credit history when making underwriting decisions.

For example, you and I are the same age, we live in the same zip code, and we are buying identical cars. Your quote is significantly lower because you have excellent credit history, whereas my quote is much higher because my credit is not great. Finance managers discuss monthly budgets with customers and therefore need to have a good idea of what it means to budget. Having bad credit is proof that budgeting is not one of the job applicant's strengths.

Now let's move on to drug tests. Make sure your dealership requires drug tests. Do not just test for cocaine and heroin; test for prescription drugs as well. There is an opioid epidemic in the country and your dealership must test for prescription drugs. If the applicant tests positive, ask him to provide a prescription. If they cannot provide a prescription, that means that they are obtaining these drugs on the black market. There is no need to hire finance managers with a prescription-drug problem. Like I said before, there are plenty of talented people there.

Another best practice is to conduct an asset check on both your finance managers and your senior management team. If all of a sudden you see one of your finance managers buying a mansion in Beverly Hills or a yacht, that should raise a red flag.

Once the background checks, drug tests, and asset checks are completed, you want to make sure that the applicant has the necessary experience and training. And that means checking references. Unfortunately, a lot of car dealers do not check references at all. Here is an interesting statistic from Monster.com:

"Desperate times often call for desperate measures—and in a brutal employment market, some job seekers may be tempted to falsify their work or education history in order to make themselves more attractive to potential employers. HireRight.com, a provider of on-demand employment background screening, found that 34 percent of job applicants lie on resumes."

We live in a litigious society and often it seems pointless to contact previous employers, because all they will tell you are the dates of employment. Therefore, I suggest contacting lenders. Lenders are usually familiar with most finance managers in the area and can tell you if the applicant submits clean deals or engages in credit application falsification, used car power booking, payment packing, or jamming of F&I products. We will discuss these noncompliant and unethical practices in the Compliance section.

During the interview, ask the applicant about her back-end gross profit generation at her previous job. If the answer seems unrealistic (let's say, $2,500 per copy), it doesn't mean she is that good; it means she is lying and misleading customers. Steer clear.

Another best practice is to ask the applicant to go through his entire presentation. A true professional will be able to do so without hesitation.

You also want to make sure that the applicant understands the importance of compliance and has previous compliance training and certification. The Association of Finance and Insurance Professionals has a very thorough certification that covers federal and state-specific regulations, as well as ethics. Also, Total Dealer Compliance offers extensive online training for new hires and existing employees in all departments.

Once you decide to hire an applicant, it is absolutely mission-critical for you to explain the culture of your organization and the behavior that you expect. Make sure your new finance manager understands your policies and procedures to avoid misunderstandings. A clear job description is the key. This may seem elementary, but it is not. The concept is foundational and works to both define and align operations throughout the organization.

Also, you need to be clear about behaviors that are not going to be tolerated. For example, you might have a one-strike-and-you're-out policy regarding falsifying credit applications. You need to be very clear about your expectations.

Effective staff development is based on clear job descriptions. This approach will help avoid confusion when it comes to job responsibilities. I see many instances where there is no clarity regarding who is supposed to perform a particular function. For example, who follows up with customers who declined to purchase F&I products—the F&I department or the BDC department? Clear job descriptions eliminate any such confusion.

Having an effective onboarding process is really important for any successful organization. Please check out our library of online courses designed for all employees of a car dealership. Through www.totaldealerompliance.com, we offer courses for Sales, BDC, F&I, HR, IT, and Fixed Ops.

Realistic Profit Expectations and Compensation Plans

Now let's talk about establishing realistic profit expectations and pay plans. First, let's look at what publicly owned auto groups are averaging in F&I. Below are the numbers published by AutoNation, the largest publicly held auto group in the country. These numbers are for the 2015 fiscal year:

> "AutoNation's F&I operations, or what the group refers to as Customer Financial Services, lived above $1,500 in F&I gross profit per vehicle retailed (PVR) in 2015, with the business unit's full-year revenues rising by $100.5 million from 2014.
>
> The group's F&I operation's full-year PVR average was $1,538, up $124 from 2014. For the fourth quarter, the business unit's PVR average came in at $1,556, up $109 from 2014's end-of-year quarter. These numbers are slightly higher for 2018 and 2019."

This is a good industry benchmark to target. The question is, how do you get there? Back-end profit comprises finance reserve and upsell of F&I products, such as service contracts, GAP, Key Replacement, etc.

One way to hit your target is to require certain product penetration. First, your dealership needs to decide what products count towards the penetration. For example, you might count only paper products, such as service contracts, pre-paid maintenance, etc.; or you might also include accessories. Once you determine what products count towards penetration, you will need to look at historical data going back at least twelve months to figure out existing product penetration. Now you are ready to set up a realistic product penetration requirement and to begin increasing it slowly. For example, you might start out at 125%

(1.25 products per deal), increasing it slowly by 5% until you get to 175%.

To reduce cancellations and customer complaints, it is a good idea to set up a maximum selling price for each product. Better yet, it is advisable to go to a one-price model for all F&I products. There is no reason for customer A to pay more than customer B for an identical product. For example, a $250 mark-up on each F&I product means that a finance manager will have to sell three products per to average $750 per deal and another $750 per deal from finance reserve. This approach prevents price gouging.

Now let's discuss pay plans. It is important to design easy-to-understand pay plans. Nobody likes changes in pay, and dealership employees are no different. Unfortunately, it has become almost a standard operating procedure for dealer principals to change pay plans. This is demoralizing and unacceptable, and it leads to employee dissatisfaction and turnover.

Your HR director, together with senior management, need to design clear and easy-to-understand pay plans and bonus plans for all employees and then stick to them.

I am big fan of motivational pay plans that pay on both product penetration and gross profit. In addition, I would add additional points for excellent customer service and timely funding of deals. As I mentioned before, it is okay to overpay great employees. For example, in New York City, finance managers get paid between 13% and 18%, and really good ones get 20%. Just imagine what kind of talent your dealership could attract if you were willing to pay 25% or even 30%. Just imagine the reduction in turnover that would result. According to Forbes, for decades, experts in talent management have emphasized the costs that are produced by turnover. It is usually said that, depending upon the complexity of the job and the level of management, the cost of turnover can equal anywhere from one month's to several years' salary for a departing employee. The more complex the job, the higher level the job, the greater the cost.

Due to the costs associated with turnover, you should monitor turnover and reduce it to a minimum. This can be accomplished by paying higher wages and having a satisfied workforce.

In addition, employees who are paid more than their peers in other dealerships will value the job much more and strive to do the right thing at all times.

Another way to stimulate product penetration and provide additional income opportunities for finance managers is to pay incentives for each product sold. Or you can set up a floating incentive—that's an incentive that is paid on a particular product for a set period of time. This approach ensures that every product gets its fair share in the presentation.

The main takeaway here is that it is okay to overpay for talent.

Selecting the Right F&I Vendor

Now let's shift our focus and discuss F&I vendors. Every dealership works with an F&I vendor, and I want to dedicate this section to choosing the right one. The F&I vendor should be an integral part of a successful finance department.

There are three types of F&I vendors—big box companies such as JM&A and Zurich, smaller independent general agents, and Original Equipment Manafucturers (OEMs). Companies such as JM&A and Zurich put up one hell of a presentation when they fly in a team of guys in suits. Unfortunately, you won't ever see them again. Dealers end up being serviced by inexperienced account reps who usually get promoted or reassigned to a different territory. Therefore, there is no continuity of service, not to mention the sky-high administration fees.

Smaller independent agents also fall into two categories. The first category is what I call "accidental agents"— those who became agents by accident because they are friends with the dealer principal. In most cases, these guys have never worked in the car business and really don't understand it. Therefore, they can't provide quality training or bring income-development ideas to the table.

The second category is a tiny minority, but these guys really know what they are doing, and working with them can make a huge difference. They have prior dealership experience as GMs or directors of finance, and they understand the business. They will provide quality training, set benchmarks, and hold finance managers accountable. They offer excellent income-development solutions, as well as help with the implementation of those solutions.

I strongly suggest that dealer principals closely examine and assess who their F&I vendors are and what they bring to the table.

OEMs such as Nissan recognize that F&I is a great way to generate additional revenue, and so they aggressively market F&I products to their dealers. OEMs incentivize dealers through additional trunk money and reduced interest rates on the floor plan. But OEMs do not have the necessary expertise. I have been doing F&I consulting for many years and can say that with absolute certainty. *F&I is not just about products, but training and motivating.* Third-party solutions coupled with an effective general agent will always produce better results.

It is important to vet F&I products to make sure that these products are approved by state insurance departments and that they are properly underwritten. Moreover, F&I vendors should never be solely responsible for the training of finance managers or for F&I compliance. There is an inherent conflict of interest, since F&I providers make money through the sale of F&I products and might look the other way when it comes to noncompliant behavior or practices. At the very minimum, I recommend that F&I providers be AFIP certified. Not to muddy the water, but the best practice is to employ an independent compliance auditor to ensure adherence to the relevant rules and regulations. Last but not least, make sure that your F&I vendor has prior F&I or dealership management experience.

If you have any questions regarding F&I training, products, and income development, do not hesitate to contact me at www. MaxZanan.com

Selecting the Right Mix of F&I Products

Now let's move on to the F&I products. What products should your dealership offer? Here are the most essential products that every dealership should offer:

- Service Contracts

- GAP

- Tire and Wheel Protection

- Paint & Fabric Protection

- Key Replacement

- Lease Wear & Tear

- Paintless Dent Repair

- Antitheft Protection

- Vehicle Sanitizing (relevant due to COVID-19)

- Vehicle Return Program (relevant due to COVID-19)

These are retention-based products that require customers to return to the dealership. Tie-back is another excellent strategy. Tie-back requires customers to come back to the dealership's service department for all repairs, as long as the breakdown is within a predefined radius, typically within fifty miles of the selling dealership. This approach is a great way to control claims and to load your shop.

A disappearing deductible is another great strategy to ensure that customers come back to the dealership's service department. Basically, there is a $0 deductible if the customer comes back to the selling dealer vs. a $200 or $300 deductible if the customer goes somewhere else.

Finance managers who have excellent product knowledge will be able to explain to the customer the beauty of a disappearing deductible.

Similar to salespeople having walk-around competitions, I want to encourage you to do the same for the finance department. Ask each finance manager to do a thorough presentation of each product they sell. You might find that some managers are uncomfortable presenting some of these products; and that could be why product penetration is not where you want it to be.

Preload Programs

Now let's shift gears and talk about preloading and upselling F&I products.

In order to improve your dealership's bottom line and remain relevant in the digital age, it is important to consider two main factors: (1) how to set yourself apart from the competition, and (2) where to focus your efforts to increase profit margins.

When devising a solid strategy to accomplish these objectives, it's crucial to identify universal trends in consumers' retail preferences and align your dealership's sales techniques appropriately. Management must also continually think outside of the box to come up with tactics that position its salespeople most optimally in the eyes of their customers.

The Value of Preinstalled Add-Ons

This is not an easy task, but to be successful, every dealership must find a way to address and conquer these challenges. One way to achieve increased income is by preinstalling low-cost items that are perceived by consumers as high value, thus positioning the items as complementary add-ons. These items include:

- Dealer-branded prepaid maintenance, which guarantees a customer will come back to the selling dealer's service department to perform scheduled maintenance. Crucially, this maintenance plan can only be used at the selling dealer, unlike OEM prepaid maintenance, which can be used at any dealership.

- Exterior paint protection, which helps keep the car looking new and increases its trade-in value.

- Interior anitimicrobial treatment is a must in the age of COVID-19.

- Engine for Life or Powertrain for Life, which ensures that customers come back to the selling dealer for all scheduled maintenance according to the owner's manual.

- Walkaway Vehicle Return Program is another must in the age of COVID-19. It allows the customer to walkaway from the car loan/lease in case of a lif-changing event such as the loss of employement.

- Antitheft protection, which is valuable because car theft is still a prevalent crime in many areas.

The Importance of Up-Selling

To offset the cost of the preload, a dealership's F&I department must be able to up-sell the exterior paint protection and prepaid maintenance to longer terms, and the antitheft protection to a greater dollar amount. To do so, a dealership's senior management team should set a certain up-sell penetration requirement to incentivize its sales teams.

Adding these items to an overall comprehensive sales strategy will undoubtedly create a sense of loyalty, cultivate a more positive opinion of the dealership, and improve profit margins.

Draw Attention to the Add-Ons

Dealers should also prominently display a separate addendum sticker to highlight the items that are included in the sale price of the car. Sales staff should be trained to fully understand the value of the add-ons, which in turn will better position them with customers.

The information featured on the addendum stickers should also be included in a dealership's print and online marketing (website, TV, radio, Internet, and social media). There should also be marketing materials on every salesperson's desk to reinforce the message.

Dealerships cannot implement a one-size-fits-all approach, however. The items mentioned here are just a few examples of the types of innovations that dealerships must implement in order to stay competitive in the ever-changing marketplace. But beware. With dealerships rushing to stand out, many implement tactics without properly validating their customers' needs first, leading to hit-or-miss results. By focusing on the universal benefits of these added perks and low-cost items, dealerships eliminate any risk of failure.

Often the car sales process begins online, but there is still a strong need for brick-and-mortar auto dealerships. By showcasing new, innovative ways to stay competitive, dealerships can adapt to changing customer needs and improve their bottom line. It is a good idea to reinsure the preloaded products because of tax advantages and reduction in commissionable gross profit.

Dealer-Branded Prepaid Maintenance

Let's examine dealer-branded, prepaid maintenance programs in greater detail. Prepaid maintenance guarantees a flow of customers coming back to the service department. These visits allow service advisors to build relationships with customers and eventually up-sell them the necessary maintenance and repair work.

Let's look at prepaid maintenance from the income-development perspective. There are two types of prepaid maintenance that dealers offer: OEM or their own. The modern dealership only offers its own prepaid maintenance.

OEM maintenance comes from the manufacturer and is good at any dealership. For example, if you sell Honda maintenance, your customers can use it at any Honda dealership in the United States.

If the customer doesn't use her prepaid maintenance, then breakage is kept by the OEM and becomes their profit, meaning the premium that your dealership paid for prepaid maintenance is kept by the manufacturer.

With a dealer-owned prepaid maintenance, the dealer designs the program and hires a third party to administer it. The main advantages of this approach are:

- Customers can only use the prepaid maintenance at the selling dealership, therefore increasing service retention.

- Customers are actively contacted to make sure that they come to redeem their services. Good program administrators can increase customer retention up to 75%. This allows service advisers to build relationships with customers and eventually up-sell required maintenance and repair work.

- The breakage is returned to the dealer and becomes additional profit.

Your dealership may want to give away the first year maintenance to enhance the Why Buy From Us story, offsetting the cost by requiring a certain upsell penetration in F&I.

Feel free to contact me if you have any questions regarding the set-up of dealer-branded, pre-paid maintenance program.

Reinsurance of F&I Products

Now let's talk about reinsurance and what it means to your bottom line.

I am amazed at how many dealers are not reinsuring their service contract business or some of their ancillary products. Reinsurance is an excellent source of income and a great tax strategy. Reinsurance allows a dealer to earn underwriting profits, plus any investment income that is earned on these premiums.

A great strategy is to create white-label service contracts and white-label ancillary products. Don't take my word for it—AutoNation did it and their F&I profits are up!

This approach helps increase customer service and retention. More importantly, it is an excellent way to improve branding at your dealership.

The best way to maximize your personal wealth outside of directly increasing F&I profitability is by owning a properly structured reinsurance company. You can increase your personal wealth immediately by optimizing your reinsurance company's structure. With your own reinsurance company, you own an asset outside the dealership and outside of factory control. Below are the main takeaways from Portfolio, the leader in dealer reinsurance solutions.

- All funds are held in your financial institution, with your chosen investment banker.

- You have 100% investment control; you choose how to invest, including floor plan offset account, stocks, bonds, mutual funds, etc.

- You can borrow up to 75% of unearned premium and 100% of your earned premium.

- Your dealership nets claims and cancellations prior to remittance.

- Service retention is guaranteed through a 40 mile tie-back. Our claims service directs your customers back through to your service department, controlling claims costs, increasing fixed ops profits, and increasing customer satisfaction.

- Your company is funded five days after receipt and as often as weekly, maximizing investment income potential.

- You can choose your risk levels for each product: self-insured, partial or full.

- You can customize rates and F&I plans depending on regional needs and market.

- Every reinsured product is segregated into separate, stand-alone trust accounts, with no commingling.

- You are provided a detailed analysis of your company's performance by product reinsured and analyzed at every level, including salesperson and service department.

- No hidden fees, No loss adjustment expense, No investment management fees, No loss of investment income.

Now let's shift gears again and discuss the fact that the F&I department is not a standalone entity.

Working with The Service Department

Your F&I department and your service department must work together so that your service-and-parts director knows what products are being sold and how to file a claim. Regular meetings should be held between your service-and-parts director and your director of finance. If service advisors do not know how to file a claim or do not want to be bothered with third-party service contracts and ancillary products, your finance department will lose credibility, and it will only be harder to sell these products in the future.

Also, it is a good idea to sell service contracts in the service drive, or at the very minimum have service advisors refer customers to the F&I Department.

In order to sell service contracts in the service drive, make sure to sign up with a 0% APR financing company, because most customers cannot afford to pay in full. Again, it is all about removing friction and making it easy for your customers.

Vendors

The Zero Plan. www.thezeroplan.com
Automotive, Power Sports, RV, Mobile Home, Exotic, New Home

- Funding within 7 Business Days

- 100% Refund of Fees in First 60 Days for Cancellations

- No Limit on Retailer Profit

- Low Cancellations - Low Chargebacks - We Collect!

- Other Ancillary Products are Eligible - Not Just Service Contracts

- Industry First-Sales Tool To Drive Revenue from Cash Buyers or Service Drive

Displaying F&I Products Online

F&I — Don't Keep It A Secret

Now let's focus on digital retail and what it means for the finance department.

According to the inaugural Car Buyer Journey study commissioned by Autotrader and conducted by HIS Automotive, as of 2016, more than 60% of the car buying process happens online. For many people, the entire car shopping process, minus the test drive, happens online. The millennial generation is placing more and more emphasis on digital communication, and that's not likely to change.

Unfortunately, the automotive industry is dragging its heels when it comes to seamless and convenient online buying methods for today's consumers. It's becoming more and more essential for dealerships to offer finance information and add-ons online, and consumers are going to turn their attention elsewhere if they don't find the information they want.

The F&I Department

The standard Finance and Insurance department—which is where the real money flows through the dealership—is seriously behind with online offerings to potential clients. F&I is where the money is made. F&I is responsible for obtaining financing and upselling service contracts and ancillary products that include Tire and Wheel Protection, GAP, Key Replacement. Thus, F&I is quite simply the profit center.

Given how seamless online car purchasing is, today's consumer is dissatisfied with the current in-dealership process because of the high-pressure sales tactics associated with it. People don't want the same sales tactic from 30-years ago; they're into a new kind of consumption—one that is digital.

How Do We Change F&I for the Digital World?

For starters, it's time to bring F&I out of the shadows and into the spotlight. Auto dealers shouldn't keep it a "secret" anymore. The best way to address the issue is through transparency. The F&I products and add-ons need to be presented on the dealer's website, front and center. Since 60% of the car-shopping process is happening on computers and mobile devices, this is where prospective consumers begin perusing various products.

Consumers want full disclosure; they want information presented to them directly and accurately online. Therefore, dealers should showcase all available information, including features, benefits, as well as prices from the get-go. People don't want to be led in a sales circle anymore. Why? Because they can just open a new tab and peruse the next dealership down the block.

This new approach can increase acceptance rates and customer satisfaction tenfold. Currently, when customers visit dealership websites, they can view a car price, schedule an appointment, and buy parts. One thing they can't do is access information about F&I products and pricing.

Don't Keep It A Secret

In this digital transparency age, keeping things a secret doesn't work anymore. It will build up frustration and distrust with consumers. Instead, embrace your F&I offerings by being upfront with consumers from the moment they open your website. By having access to this information, they'll be more inclined to include the add-ons with their final purchase, as well as share the information with friends and family.

Understanding Proper Workload

Now let's talk about work-life balance. Below is the quote from menthalhealthamerica.net:

> "While we all need a certain amount of stress to spur us on and help us perform at our best, the key to managing stress lies in that one magic word: balance. Not only is achieving a healthy work/life balance an attainable goal but workers and businesses alike see the rewards. When workers are balanced and happy, they are more productive, take fewer sick days, and are more likely to stay in their jobs."

The car business is guilty of burning people out due to the grueling schedule, and that's one of the main reasons it is hard to attract the right personnel. I am a big believer in the 5-day workweek. This approach allows finance managers to focus on getting customers approved, getting deals funded, and most importantly spending enough quality time with customers. Seeing an average of 3 to 3.5 customers per work day will ensure a quality interaction with customers and enough time to present products and build value. If your finance managers are taking more than 80 turns per month, then your dealership is burning them out and you are leaving money on the table.

Menu Presentation

When it comes to presenting F&I products in the dealership, menu presentation is the best approach. There are great menus available, such as MaximTrak, that easily integrate with Reynolds & Reynolds, ADP, and other smaller Dealer Management Systems.

The finance department is tasked with obtaining the most favorable financing options for the customer, as well as maximizing profitability by selling F&I products. Often I find that there is no uniform process when it comes to this critical profit center. Dealers rely on the best efforts of their finance managers, instead of focusing on a standardized process and performance benchmarks. Product penetration percentages and PVR are not mentioned in the finance manager's job description, and dealers simply hope for the best. When properly used, menu selling is the most effective tool to ensure that 100% of products are presented 100% of the time to 100% of the customers.

Most sophisticated dealers use electronic menus that integrate with DMS software; however, installing a menu system is not enough. It is absolutely critical to implement effective policies and procedures in order to obtain the desired outcome. Below are the most effective policies and procedures using the DMAIC process. DMAIC is the core tool used in Six Sigma projects.

- **Define** the objective. The dealer principal or general manager must state what the desired PVR and product penetration percentages are.

- **Measure**. Start by measuring the last twelve months of production in order to account for seasonal changes.

- **Analyze**. Assess what products are being sold, as well as the average gross profit and penetration for each product.

- **Improve**. Set a desired PVR and product penetration, and train finance managers to effectively present the menu.

Implement a pay plan that incentivizes finance managers to perform at the optimum level.

— **Control**. Review and incrementally increase desired outcome on a monthly or quarterly basis.

It is essential that there is a fail-safe mechanism to make sure that finance managers are using the menu. I recommend not billing a deal unless there is a signed menu. Another approach is to use a menu that monitors the key strokes. This way, the dealer will know how much time the finance manager spent presenting each product. Following these steps will allow the finance department to increase product penetration and gross profit, while increasing customer retention.

Vendors

Maxim Trak. www.maximtrak.com

MaximTrak is strategically designed to align F&I best practices and industry knowledge with cutting-edge technology, helping to transform a dealership's F&I department into a powerful profit center. With this all-in-one interactive menu-selling system, dealerships can close more business and streamline successful, repeatable processes while significantly enhancing the car buying experience.

Unsold Customer Follow-Up

Unfortunately, most finance managers do not engage in any unsold follow-ups after the customer leaves their office. These finance managers (and their dealerships) are missing out on a tremendous profit center. It is common for customers to pass on purchasing products, and dealers should follow up at a later time to try again. This strategy is guaranteed to increase product penetration. Follow-up should include an email and a phone call campaign. The dealership has to decide whether finance managers or BDC staff will do this follow up.

In addition, there are third parties that sell vehicle service contracts on behalf of the dealership directly to consumers. You give them access to your customer database, and they contact customers whose vehicle service contract or factory warranty is about to expire. Your dealership receives commission for each contract sold. This is a great way to generate additional revenue without investing a penny or changing any of your processes.

By working with third party companies, you can be assured that expiring service contracts will be identified and those customers contacted. You absolutely must be in that space!

Vendors

Darwin Automotive. www.darwinautomotive.com
In just a few steps, your customers can purchase previously declined F&I products right from their phone.

Smooth Cancellation Process

Now let's shift gears again and discuss cancellations. Cancellations are part of the business, and it is essential to have a smooth cancellation process in your F&I department.

Customers occasionally need to cancel F&I products, and the cancellation process in many dealerships is not straightforward. These dealerships are guilty of giving the customer a runaround, and that's unacceptable. In most cases, there would be no need to cancel products if customers were properly informed in the first place. So training your finance managers on all products is essential. For cancellations that cannot be avoided, there must be a clear, written cancellation/refund process, and every finance manager has to follow it.

F&I Takeaways

Nationwide (prior to Covid-19) auto retail sales are at the highest level, and dealers are targets of investigations by state and federal agencies. To help your dealership preserve your income and reputation, you must maintain a compliant F&I department. Achieving this involves several factors:

- Background checks, drug tests, and references for all finance managers

- Certification and ongoing training of all service managers

- An effective onboarding process; clear, thorough policies and procedures

- F&I product and vendor assessment

- Clearly defined product penetration requirements and profit expectations

F&I is an extremely important department, and it is paramount that you hire the right people, that you train them, and that you set realistic expectations. In addition, F&I is where dealers make the lion's share of their money. A great F&I department uses a menu, reinsures F&I products, and has multiple preloads. It is important to understand that an improperly run F&I department can cause tremendous losses (financial and reputational) through noncompliant and unethical practices. Today's progressive dealership employs a compliance officer and has strong internal controls.

4
F&I COMPLIANCE

IN THIS CHAPTER we will cover setting up an effective and robust compliance program in the Finance Department. A truly great finance department adheres to the code of ethics and does not engage in noncompliant business practices.

In this course we will review the following topics:

- Change in consumer buying habits

- Benefits of a compliance program

- Hiring the right finance managers

- Components of a successful compliance program

- Proactive state and federal regulators

- Organizational culture

- Appointing a compliance officer

- Independent 3rd party audits

- Online compliance courses
- Important rules and regulations that affect the finance department
- Safeguards Rule
  - ✓ Disposal Rule
  - ✓ Privacy Rule
  - ✓ Red Flags Rule
  - ✓ OFAC
  - ✓ Form 8300
  - ✓ TILA/CLA
- Fair Credit Compliance Program
- F&I product uniform pricing
- Risk-based pricing
- Adverse Action Notice
- Major risks associated with finance department
  - ✓ Falsifying credit applications
  - ✓ Power booking
  - ✓ Payment packing
  - ✓ Jamming F&I products
- Steps to reduce compliance risks
- Displaying F&I products online
- Consequences of unethical and noncompliant practices
- Two major reasons why a robust compliance program is a must

We live in the age of Amazon and Uber and that means we are used to convenience and transparency. Here's what I mean: When you order a product on Amazon, you know exactly how much you paid for it and when it is going to be delivered. When you order an Uber, you know when the car is going to be in front of your house and how much will it cost to go from point A to point B. It is only logical and natural for consumers to expect this level of transparency when shopping for a car or F&I products.

Transparency and compliance go hand-in-hand, and therefore it is crucial to have a robust compliance program in the F&I department.

The compliance program that we are going to cover in this chapter is based on Federal Regulations. Federal Regulations are the foundation for state and local regulations, and therefore every dealership, at the very minimum, must design and implement a compliance program that adheres to federal regulations.

Another reason for having a robust compliance program is to improve the overall reputation of car dealers. According to a Gallup Poll, members of Congress, lobbyists, and car salesmen edged out telemarketers for having the worst reputations for honesty and ethical standards.

Bad reputations, coupled with customer complaints, is the reason federal and state regulators go after car dealers on a regular basis. These investigations result in newspaper headlines that in turn contribute to the worsening reputation of car dealers. In addition, these investigations generate hundreds of thousands and even millions of dollars in fines and penalties.

The success of any compliance program depends on the organizational culture and talent that it attracts. Compliance and ethical behavior start at the top. The dealer principal and senior management team must set the tone and clearly articulate what the organizational culture and mission is. And in turn, the customers win because they're getting great service from highly motivated employees.

An integral part of any compliance program is an audit by an independent 3rd party to determine the baseline. Total Dealer

Compliance provides onsite compliance audits that help uncover problems and reduce risk, as well as improve internal controls.

Audits consist of interviews with the dealer principal and members of the senior management team, and a review of policies and procedures, training, and processes. Total Dealer Compliance provides a report that outlines the necessary steps to elevate the level of compliance, as well as a list of Best Practices.

Next is the appointment of a compliance officer. The same way dealers appoint sales and service managers, they need to appoint a compliance officer to oversee enforcement of policies and procedures, internal auditing, and training. In most stand-alone dealerships, the comptroller or the CFO is best suited for this position. Larger auto groups should have a dedicated, full-time compliance officer.

I briefly mentioned having clear policies and procedures. Let's explore this topic in greater detail.

Policies and procedures must specify what behavior is not going to be tolerated. Most dealers do not have **any** written policies and procedures. There might be an employee handbook, which no one ever reads. It all starts with effective HR and operational policies and onboarding. Here is what usually happens—new hires are handed a stack of papers to sign, and they sign them on autopilot without ever reading a single page. Total Dealer Compliance has an online platform with over 25 courses, and there is a test at the end of each course. This approach ensures that that there is an electronic paper trail and employees actually read the necessary policies and procedures.

Safeguards Rule

Now let's review the most relevant regulations that every finance department must comply with. First, we will focus on Safeguards Rule.

The Safeguards Rule requires financial institutions under FTC jurisdiction to have measures in place to keep customer information secure. In addition, companies covered by the Rule are responsible for taking steps to ensure that their affiliates and service providers safeguard customer information in their care.

Sensitive customer information is necessarily provided as part of financial transaction, and this includes:

- Financial, credit data
- Social security number
- Birth date
- Mother's maiden name; other names used
- Family data
- Religion, race, national origin
- Performance ratings
- Account numbers

Safeguards Rule has been in effect since May 23rd of 2003. I can tell you from experience that most dealers do not have an effective Safeguards program in place, even though the rule has been in effect for such a long time.

FTC fines are pretty severe—$11,000 per day, per occurrence, so this alone is a good enough reason to focus your efforts on the Safeguards Rule.

Car dealers tend to think that they will never be victims of a data breach. This is faulty thinking. Every dealership is a treasure trove of nonpublic information, and hackers know that. So it is not a question of if, but a question of when.

Total Dealer Compliance conducted a survey and here is what we found:

- Just under 84% of consumers will not go back to buy another vehicle from a dealership after their data has been compromised.

- More than 70% of dealers are not up to date on their anti-virus software.

- Only 30% of dealers employ a network engineer with computer security certifications/training.

- Only 25% hired a third-party vendor to try to hack into their networks to test their vulnerability.

These are alarming statistics.

In order for your finance department to have a robust compliance program, your compliance officer must conduct a physical and electronic threat assessment on a regular basis.

Let's talk about physical security and social engineering. This is an important part of the threat assessment. Most hackers do not just try to penetrate a computer network remotely, because in many instances, it is easier to just walk in and take whatever they need. I have been to too many dealerships where there are no doors in the F&I offices, let alone locks. I have visited dealerships where there were doors but no locks, or there were locks but no keys. A lot of dealerships still don't have shredders.

Another important aspect of physical security is access control. For example, in most dealerships salespeople have full access to the F&I office. Trust me: there is no reason for that.

It is mission-critical to implement effective access control, and that means doors, electronic access cards instead of old-fashioned locks, and closed-circuit television. And pay special attention to securing your server room.

Even though this section is dedicated to Safeguards Rule, we need to briefly discuss Disposal Rule. Disposal Rule governs how you dispose of customer information, and that means you need to have a procedure for disposing of paper files and electronic files. I strongly suggest you use a third-party shredding service for paper disposal and a computer security firm that will wipe the hard drives before you dispose of obsolete technology.

Now let's talk about social engineering. Social engineering is the art of manipulating people so they give up confidential information. The types of information criminals are seeking can vary, but when individuals are targeted, the criminals are usually trying to trick them into providing their passwords or bank information, or into giving full access to their computer.

Employees need to be vigilant about not sharing any sensitive information. Effective onboarding of new employees and regular training of existing employees is the foundation to prevent social engineering attacks.

Now let's talk about threat assessment and how it relates to computer security.

According to Dealertrack, in the last 12 months, 71% of small to midsize businesses reported a security breach, and most of those could be attributed to the actions of employees and vendors or to a lack of security on the premises.

That means that dealers need to pay close attention to their employees. It is a good idea to set up a centrally managed password change procedure, limit access to information, install email monitoring software, update anti-virus software, limit internet access, and disable USB ports.

In case of a termination, it is critical that you terminate the employee's logins and disable access cards. It's also a good idea to conduct an exit interview to make sure that you part ways on amicable terms. Let's review these recommendations in greater detail.

I am a big believer in limiting employees' internet access. First, there is no need for fantasy football or National Geographic during work hours. Also, my suggestion is to limit the cell phone use.

Second, employees sometimes inadvertently download viruses that will jeopardize data and the productivity of your organization.

It is also a good idea to monitor employee emails. There are some basic email surveillance solutions available that help monitor employee emails to ensure critical data isn't being inadvertently, or purposely, shared. While the federal government doesn't place restrictions on employee internet monitoring, some individual states have put protections in place. An increasing number of states require employers to notify their workers if their company monitors online activity, including emails and keystrokes. These notifications can be disclosed within the employee handbook, as part of the new worker orientation or simply sent out as an email reminder to employees.

USB ports must be disabled because they pose a dual threat. First, an employee might bring an infected USB drive to work and inadvertently damage the dealership's network. Second, a disgruntled employee might download enterprise data to get back at his or her employer.

I strongly suggest that you hire a 3rd party to test your network. These engineers act like hackers and try to break into your network. They identify vulnerabilities and provide a report on how to secure your network. Total Dealer Compliance provides this type of service.

Unfortunately, hackers are becoming more and more sophisticated, and there is a chance that even if you implement the most reasonable steps to protect data, your dealership might be hacked. Therefore, it is extremely important to have comprehensive cyber insurance.

In a May 2017 survey from the Council of Insurance Agents and Brokers, only 32% of U.S. businesses had some type of cyber insurance. And many of those do not have full coverage.

When shopping for cyber insurance, consider the following factors and coverage:

- Direct monetary loss through electronic theft

- Losses due to extortion from DDoS blackmail or ransomware

- Costs of mitigating and investigating the incident

- Losses due to downtime

- Losses from damage to data and systems, and the costs associated with restoring systems back to normal

- Costs of remediation, including the cost to improve security and prevent a similar breach going forward

- The cost of customer breach notification, including legal costs and public relations

- Expenses from customer compensation, including credit monitoring, service-level agreement penalties, refunds and contractual breaches

- Costs of liability associated with the breach, including legal costs

In the event of a data breach, your dealership needs to know what steps to take, and that's why it is a good idea to develop a Data Breach Protocol.

Your Data Breach Protocol should (1) designate a spokesperson, (2) identify a mechanism to notify all affected individuals, (3) update the website, (4) alert the media, and (5) contact the insurance company.

Now let's keep going with practical steps to safeguard your customers' nonpublic information.

Safeguard Rule requires that your dealership develop a written information security program. A critical part of this written program is overseeing your vendors and service providers. A typical dealership has about 30 different vendors plugged into the DMS, so you need to make sure that your service providers take safeguarding customer information seriously; ask them for copies of recent security audits. Also, make sure that there is data security clause in the contract that obligates the vendor to safeguard your customers' nonpublic information. Once you decide to stop using a vendor for any reason, make sure that all the DMS connections are terminated.

It's important to note that this is not a one-time deal. Compliance, and especially compliance with the Safeguard Rule, is an ongoing process, and that means that you have to update your program on regular basis and train your employees accordingly. And please document these training sessions. Remember, if it is not documented, it never happened.

Red Flags Rule

Now that we've covered Safeguards and Disposal Rule, let's move onto the Red Flags Rule. First, a little history about the Red Flags Rule.

The **Red Flags Rule** was created by the Federal Trade Commission (FTC), along with other government agencies such as the National Credit Union Administration (NCUA), to help prevent identity theft. The rule applies to two different entities: financial institutions and creditors.

Financial institution is defined as a state or national bank, a state or federal savings and loan association, a mutual savings bank, a state or federal credit union, or any other entity that holds a "transaction account" belonging to a consumer.

Creditor is defined as any entity that regularly extends or renews credit—or arranges for others to do so—and includes all entities that regularly permit deferred payments for goods or services.

The definition of a **creditor** was further clarified by the Red Flag Program Clarification Act of 2010. Under the Clarification Act, a **creditor** regularly and in the course of business:

- Obtains or uses consumer credit reports,

- Provides information to consumer reporting agencies, OR

- Advances funds that must be repaid in the future (or against collateral).

This rule applies to many different types of businesses, and automobile dealers is one of them. Why? Because an automobile dealer "advances funds or routinely interacts with consumer credit agencies when performing a service and receiving payment once the work is complete."

Elements of Red Flags Rule

The Red Flags Rule tells you how to develop, implement, and administer an identity-theft prevention program. The program must include four basic elements :

1. The program must include reasonable policies and procedures to identify the red flags of identity theft that may occur in your day-to-day operations. Red Flags are suspicious patterns or practices, or specific activities that indicate the possibility of identity theft. For example, if a customer has to provide some form of identification to open an account with your company, an ID that doesn't look genuine is a "red flag" for your business.

2. The program must be designed to detect the red flags you've identified. If you have identified fake IDs as a red flag, for example, you must have procedures to detect possible fake, forged, or altered identification.

3. The program must spell out appropriate actions you'll take when you detect red flags.

4. The program must detail how you'll keep it current to reflect new threats.

First: Identify Relevant Red Flags

Risk Factors. To identify key red flags, think about the sales process in your dealership. For example, what mechanism do you have in place to determine if a driver's license is real?

Sources of Red Flags. Consider other sources of information, including the experience of other members of your industry. Technology, as well as criminal techniques, change constantly, so it's important to keep up-to-date on new threats.

The examples below may help you identify red flags that are relevant to your business.

- **Alerts, Notifications, and Warnings** from a Credit Reporting Company. Changes in a credit report or a consumer's credit activity might signal identity theft. These include:

  ✓ a fraud or active duty alert on a credit report

  ✓ a notice of credit freeze in response to a request for a credit report

  ✓ a notice of address discrepancy provided by a credit reporting company

  ✓ a credit report indicating a pattern inconsistent with the person's history; for example, an increase in the volume of inquiries or the use of credit, especially on new accounts; an unusual number of recently established credit relationships; an account that was closed because of an abuse of account privileges

- **Suspicious Documents**. Careful scrutiny of documents can reveal identity theft, such as:

  ✓ Identification looks altered or forged.

  ✓ The person presenting the identification doesn't look like the photo or match the physical description.

✓ The information on the identification differs from the information provided by the customer; the ID doesn't match a signature card or recent check

✓ An application looks like it's been altered, forged, or torn up and reassembled

- **Personal Identifying Information**. Inconsistent personal information can indicate identity theft.

    ✓ Inconsistencies with what you already know—for example, an address that doesn't match the credit report, or the use of a social security number that's listed on the Social Security Administration Death Master File

    ✓ Inconsistencies in the information a customer has submitted to you

    ✓ An address, phone number, or other personal information already used on an account you know to be fraudulent

    ✓ A bogus address, an address for a mail drop or prison, a phone number that's invalid or one that's associated with a pager or answering service

    ✓ A social security number used by someone else opening an account

    ✓ An address or telephone number used by several people opening accounts

    ✓ A person who omits required information on an application and doesn't respond to notices that the application is incomplete

    ✓ A person who can't provide authenticating information beyond what's generally available from a wallet or credit report—for example, someone who can't answer a challenge question

- **Account Activity**. How an account is being used can be a tip-off to identity theft.

  - ✓ A new account used in ways associated with fraud—for example, the customer doesn't make the first payment, or makes only an initial payment; or most of the available credit is used for cash advances or for jewelry, electronics, or other merchandise easily convertible to cash

  - ✓ An account used outside of established patterns—for example, nonpayment when there's no history of missed payments, a big increase in the use of available credit, or a major change in buying or spending patterns or electronic fund transfers

  - ✓ An inactive account is used

  - ✓ Information about unauthorized charges on the account

Second: Detect Red Flags

Using identity verification and authentication methods can help you detect red flags. I am a big fan of Fraud Fighter hardware. This is the same equipment that TSA agents use to determine the validity of driver's licenses.

New Accounts

When verifying the identity of the person who is opening a new account, reasonable procedures should include obtaining a name, address, social security number, and ID, such as a current government-issued identification card like a driver's license or passport. Depending on the circumstances, you may want to compare that information with other sources, like a credit reporting company or data broker, or the Social Security Number Death Master File. Asking questions based on information from other sources can be a helpful way to verify someone's identity.

Note Suspicious Behavior

Certain behavior might be a sign of a red flag. For example, if the buyer is willing to pay any price without negotiation and wants to take delivery as soon as possible, this can indicate a problem.

Third: Prevent And Mitigate Identity Theft

It is important to train sales and F&I staff on recognizing Red Flags such as a discrepancy in address, social security number, date of birth, and so on. I strongly recommend an electronic Red Flags check provided by Dealertrack and RouteOne. These companies supply an out-of-wallet questions to help finance managers establish the identity of a buyer. Out-of-Wallet questions are designed so that if someone were to steal your wallet, they could not use the information to answer any questions.

Remember: you must stop the sale if you are dealing with an identity thief. As a dealer, you guarantee the identities of all buyers, and lender agreements have language that requires you to repurchase contracts sold to identity thieves. In addition, FTC can seek $3500 per violation. So don't take the chance!

Fourth, Update The Program

The Rule recognizes that new red flags emerge as technology changes or identity thieves change their tactics, and this requires periodic updates to your program. Factor in your own experience with identity theft—changes in how identity thieves operate; new methods to detect, prevent, and mitigate identity theft; changes in the accounts you offer; and changes in your business, such as mergers, acquisitions, alliances, joint ventures, and arrangements with service providers. Identity theft is a even bigger threat during COVID-19 pandemic—your customers are wearing masks, and dealers are delivering cars to customers' homes. Make sure you have protocols in place to minimize risks. Moving forward, consider using a notary service that will be present at delivery to ensure the validity of customer documents.

Administering Dealership Red Flags Program

Your Red Flags Program must be approved by a senior manager, and a Senior Manager should oversee, develop, implement, and administer the program. Your compliance officer is best suited for this role, as responsibilities include reviewing staff reports about compliance with the Rule and approving important changes to your program.

The person responsible for your program should report at least annually to your Board of Directors or a designated senior manager. The report should evaluate how effective your program has been in addressing the risk of identity theft, how you're monitoring the practices of your service providers, significant incidents of identity theft and your response, and recommendations.

OFAC

The Office of Foreign Assets Control (OFAC) of the US Department of the Treasury administers and enforces economic and trade sanctions based on US foreign policy and national security goals against targeted foreign countries and regimes, terrorists, international narcotics traffickers, those engaged in activities related to the proliferation of weapons of mass destruction, and other threats to the national security, foreign policy or economy of the United States.

OFAC publishes the Specially Designated Nationals (SDN) List, which lists people, organizations and vessels with whom United States citizens and permanent residents are prohibited from doing business. This list is available at www.treasury.gov.

OFAC Compliance

Your dealership must appoint a compliance officer with respect to any and all issues that pertain to OFAC.

All transactions should be checked against the list of names of individuals, entities, geographical locations or countries that have been identified by OFAC. This includes (but is not limited to):

- Beneficiaries

- Collateral owners

- Guarantors/cosigners

- Receiving parties

- Sending parties

The OFAC restrictions are extremely broad, and there is no minimum dollar threshold. Therefore, the restrictions prohibit dealers from entering into a contract for a mere oil change if the customer is a "prohibited person." In other words, the restrictions don't just prohibit dealers from entering into a contract with a prohibited person for the purchase of a high-end vehicle.

If there is no match, then the transaction may proceed. If there is a potential match, you should perform additional due diligence to determine whether the match to the name on the OFAC list is an actual match or a false positive.

Any transaction that has been blocked or rejected must be reported to OFAC within ten business days.

Best Practice Tip

Dealerships should run OFAC Checks on their employees on a regular basis.

Record Retention

All OFAC related records must be kept for five years.

Each year, you must submit an annual report of all transactions blocked from July 1 of the previous year to June 30 of the current year. This report is due every September 30th.

OFAC Penalties

The penalties for noncompliance can be severe. Depending on the program, criminal penalties can include fines from $50,000 to $10 million, and imprisonment from 10 to 30 years for willful violations. Civil penalties can range from $11,000 to $1 million for each violation.

It is important for your dealership to conduct and document regular training on OFAC to mitigate risk and exposure.

Similar to Red Flags, I strongly recommend that your dealership use an OFAC software solution provided by Dealertrack or RouteOne.

Vendor Section

700Credit. www.700credit.com

Excellent resource for compliance. They provide:

1. Red Flag ID

2. Adverse Action Notice

3. Risk-Based Pricing

4. OFAC Search

5. Privacy Notice

Privacy Rule

Now let's review the Privacy Rule.

The stated purpose of the GLB Act (1999) and the FTC's Privacy Rule is to ensure that financial institutions respect the privacy of their customers and protect the security and confidentiality of "nonpublic personal information." The definition of a financial institution has been broadly interpreted and will, in most cases, include motor vehicle dealerships.

Motor vehicle dealerships that fall under the definition of a financial institution are prohibited from disclosing certain personal information about their customers to third parties unless they satisfy privacy notice and opt-out requirements.

Although the GLB Act does not prohibit a financial institution from disclosing nonpublic personal information about a consumer to affiliated parties, nor does it require a financial institution to provide a consumer with the opportunity to opt-out of such information-sharing before doing so, the FTC's Final Rule, the Fair Credit Reporting Act (FCRA), and some state laws impose additional disclosure requirements and limitations on disclosures of nonpublic information to affiliated companies.

The combined regulations require financial institutions to provide particular notices and to comply with certain limitations on disclosure of nonpublic personal information. A financial institution must provide a notice of its privacy policies and practices with respect to both affiliated and nonaffiliated third parties; and it must allow the consumer to opt out of the disclosure of the consumer's nonpublic personal information to a nonaffiliated third party if the disclosure is outside of the exceptions.

The following will provide you with a fundamental understanding of the financial privacy rules and how to follow them.

The GLB Act and the FTC's Final Rule govern *financial institutions* that collect *nonpublic personal information* about individuals who obtain a *financial product or service*.

Financial Institution. The FTC chose to retain a broad definition of financial institution. That definition encompasses retail sellers of goods if they assist consumers in obtaining credit or extend credit themselves. A motor vehicle dealership is also a financial institution if it, in the regular course of its business, leases motor vehicles on a non-operating basis for longer than 90 days.

Financial Products and Services. Like the definition of financial institution, the FTC also adopted a broad definition of financial products or services. The definition includes the *evaluation* of information collected in connection with an application by a consumer for a financial product or service, even if the application ultimately is rejected or withdrawn. It also includes the *distribution* of information about a consumer in obtaining a financial product or service. In some cases, the only product or service offered is the funding of the loan, directly or indirectly. In other cases, the product or service is the processing of payments, sending account-related notices, and responding to consumer inquiries. For example, if your dealership obtains a credit application from an individual and evaluates the information provided to determine whether or not the individual qualifies for financing, you have provided a financial product or service.

A motor vehicle dealership also provides a financial product or service if it provides a copy of the application or the information contained therein to another lending institution.

Nonpublic Personal Information. The definition here is also broad. Nonpublic personal information refers to:

- Any personally identifiable financial information that is provided by a consumer to a financial institution

- The results of any transaction with the consumer or any financial service performed for the consumer

- Information otherwise obtained by the financial institution.

Examples of nonpublic personal information include:

- Information a consumer provides on an application to obtain a loan

- Account balance information, payment history, and credit card information

- The fact that an individual is or has been one of your customers or has obtained a financial product or service from you

- Any information that a consumer provides to you that you or your agent otherwise obtain in connection with collecting on or servicing a credit account

- Any information you collect through an Internet "cookie" (an information collecting device from a web server)

- Information from a consumer report

Nonpublic personal information also includes any list, description, or other grouping of consumers that is obtained in whole or in part using any personally identifiable financial information that is not publicly available.

Information is publicly available if a financial institution has a *reasonable basis* to believe that the information is lawfully made available to the general public. In order to meet this standard, you must demonstrate that you have taken steps to determine that the information is of the type that is available to the general public. Moreover, if an individual has the right to direct that the information not be made available to the general public, you must demonstrate that the consumer is aware of the disclosure.

Compliance

In summary, you are required to comply with the notice and opt-out requirements under the GLB Act and the FTC's Final Rule if you:

- Accept a credit application from an individual, even if financing is never extended by either the motor vehicle dealership or a third party

- Enter into an agreement or understanding with an individual whereby you agree to assist the individual in obtaining a loan or credit to purchase or lease a vehicle and/or related goods or services

- Execute a contract with or extend financing to an individual for the purchase or lease of a motor vehicle and/or related goods or services (including any side agreement to finance a product or service and/or agreement for a deferred down payment)

- Assist an individual in obtaining financing for the purchase or lease of a motor vehicle and/or related goods or services, regardless of whether the finance or lease agreement is subsequently assigned to a lender or is directly between the consumer and the lender

- Insure, guarantee, or indemnify against loss, damage, illness, disability, or death; or act as principal, agent, or broker for the sale of insurance designed for any of these purposes. (Although the regulation of privacy in the insurance context is left to state insurance authorities, it is unclear whether motor vehicle dealerships will be deemed to be engaging in a financial activity when they sell motor vehicle service contracts or guaranteed automobile protection (GAP) products, which are not regulated as an insurance product. If your motor vehicle dealership is an obligor on such a product or has an affiliated insurance agency in order to sell these products, you may be engaging in a financial activity).

Motor vehicle dealerships are not required to make the GLB Act disclosures to companies or individuals who obtain financial products or services for business, commercial or agricultural purposes, although you may choose to do so as a courtesy to these types of customers. Your obligations under the GLB Act begin when you establish a "consumer" or "customer" relationship. Understanding the distinction between these two terms is essential, because the type of relationship you establish with an individual will determine your notice and opt-out obligations.

A consumer is an individual who obtains or has obtained a financial product or service from a financial institution to be used for personal, family, or household purposes, including individuals who apply for credit or provide nonpublic personal information to you, even if a loan is never extended. In fact, the FTC states that the **mere evaluation** of an application for credit qualifies as a financial product or service.

A customer is a consumer who has a *customer relationship* with you—that is, a continuing relationship.

The FTC's Final Rule provides, in part, that a consumer becomes a customer (that is, establishes a continuing relationship with you) when he:

- Obtains a loan from you

- Enters into an agreement or understanding with you whereby you undertake to arrange a loan for him

- Enters into a lease of personal property on a non-operating basis with you

- Has a loan for which you own servicing rights

- Is obligated on an account that you purchase from another financial institution, regardless of whether the account is in default when purchased (unless you do not locate the consumer or attempt to collect any amount from the consumer on the account)

- Originates a loan with you for personal, family, or household purposes

- Executes a contract to obtain credit from you or purchases insurance from you

- Executes a lease for personal property with you.

The GLB Act requires a financial institution to provide an initial notice of its privacy policies and practices in two circumstances:

1. For customers, the initial privacy notice must be provided at the time of establishing a customer relationship.

2. For consumers, the initial privacy notice must be provided prior to disclosing nonpublic personal information about the consumer to a nonaffiliated third party.

As a practical matter, motor vehicle dealerships should provide the initial privacy notice to the customer at the dealership. The notice should be provided when the dealership accepts the customer's credit application. The latest initial privacy notice should be provided is when other disclosures required by law, such as those required pursuant to the Truth in Lending and Truth in Leasing Acts, are provided to the customer.

You are not required to provide an annual privacy notice if:

- You sell, assign, or transfer all of the servicing rights in a loan or lease to another entity.

- You extend the loan to the customer and the customer pays the loan/lease in full or it is charged off.

- Financing is not extended to the customer by any entity and you cease assisting the individual in obtaining financing.

- You assist the customer in obtaining financing directly from another financial entity, and you are no longer required to provide any statements or notices to the customer concerning that relationship.

The annual notice must be provided at least once within each 12-month period, and it must be a full notice that reflects your current and anticipated privacy policies and practices for the next 12-month period.

Remember: when the customer relationship ends, you still have a consumer relationship with the individual, and you must comply with the notice and opt-out requirements with respect to that relationship.

Unless you are otherwise permitted by law to disclose non-public personal information, you may not, directly or through any affiliate, disclose any nonpublic personal information unless you have provided the initial privacy notice and a clear and conspicuous opt-out notice (that accurately explains the consumer's rights), and the individual has not opted out. (Be sure you have given the customer a reasonable opportunity to do so.) The opt-out notice may be provided together with or on the same written form as the initial privacy notice you provide to the customer. But if you choose to provide the opt-out notice at some later time, you must also include a copy of your privacy notice with the opt-out notice. Hence, to simplify this process, many dealerships combine the initial privacy notice and opt-out notice in a single form.

To create an adequate opt-out notice:

- Identify all of the categories of nonpublic personal information that you disclose or reserve the right to disclose

- Identify all of the categories of affiliates and nonaffiliated third parties to whom you disclose or reserve the right to disclose the information

- State that the consumer can opt-out of the disclosure of that information, unless the disclosure is permitted by an exception in the GLB Act, the FCRA, or the FTC's Final Rule, or is otherwise permitted by law

- Identify the financial products or services that the consumer obtains from you, either singly or jointly, to which the opt-out decision applies

- Provide a reasonable means by which the consumer may exercise his opt-out right.

Neither the GLB Act nor the FTC's Final Rule preempt or alter any state statute, regulation or order, except to the extent the state interpretation is inconsistent with the Federal Law and implementing Rules, even if it affords a consumer greater protection than is provided under the Federal Act or Rule. Therefore, you should consult with your legal counsel to determine if your state privacy requirements afford more protection to individuals in your state and whether additional disclosures are required.

Form 8300

Our next topic of discussion is Form 8300.

Generally speaking, any person in a trade or business who receives more than $10,000 in cash in a single transaction or related transactions must complete a Form 8300: Report of Cash Payments Over $10,000 Received in a Trade or Business.

Form 8300 is a joint form issued by the IRS and the Financial Crimes Enforcement Network (FinCEN) and is used by the government to track individuals who evade taxes and those who profit from criminal activities. Because auto dealerships frequently receive cash in excess of $10,000, we are required to comply with the filing requirements.

Type of Payments to Report

Trades and businesses must report cash payments received if all of the following criteria is met:

1. The amount of cash received within a 12-month period is more than $10,000.

   - The business receives the cash in one lump sum or in installment payments that total more than $10,000 within one year of the initial payment.

   - Previously unreported payments cause the total cash received within a 12-month period to total more than $10,000

2. The establishment receives the cash in the ordinary course of a trade or business.

3. The same agent or buyer provides the cash.

4. The business receives the cash in a single transaction or in related transactions.

What Does Cash Include?

Cash includes the coins and currency of the United States and of any foreign country. Cash may also include cashier's checks, bank drafts, traveler's checks, and money orders with a face value of $10,000 or less, if the business receives the instrument in a designated reporting transaction. (A designated Reporting Transaction is a retail sale, or the receipt of funds by a broker or other intermediary in connection with a retail sale, of a consumer durable, a collectible, or a travel or entertainment activity.) However, since cash of $10,000 or less need not be reported using Form 8300, "cash" in the context of reporting requirements refers to coins and currency.

Cash does not include:

- Personal checks drawn on the account of the writer

- A cashier's check, bank draft, traveler's check or money order with a face value of more than $10,000

To explain, when a customer uses currency of more than $10,000 to purchase a monetary instrument, the financial institution issuing the cashier's check, bank draft, traveler's check or money order is required to report the transaction by filing the Currency Transaction Report. Thus, you are not required to report the transaction.

Definition of a Related Transaction

The law requires that trades and businesses report transactions when customers use cash in a single transaction or a related transaction. Related transactions are transactions between a payer, or an agent of the payer, and a recipient of cash that occur within a 24-hour period. If the same payer makes two or more transactions totaling more than $10,000 in a 24-hour period, the business must treat the transactions as one transaction and report the payments. A 24-hour period is 24 consecutive hours, not necessarily a calendar day or banking day.

Required Written Statement for Customers

When a business is required to file a Form 8300, the law requires the business to provide a written statement to each person(s) named on Form 8300 to notify them that the business has filed the form. This requirement does not apply to Form 8300 that is filed voluntarily—that is, when Form 8300 is used to report a suspicious transaction involving less than $10,000.

The statement must include the following information:

- Name and address of the cash recipient's business

- Name and telephone number of a contact person for the business

- The total amount of reportable cash received in a 12-month period

- A statement that the cash recipient is reporting the information to the IRS

The business filing Form 8300 must provide its identified customers with the written statement **on or before Jan. 31** of the year that immediately follows the year the customer made the cash payment.

Reporting Suspicious Transactions

There may be situations where you are suspicious about a transaction. A transaction is suspicious if:

- It appears that a person is trying to prevent a business from filing Form 8300.

- It appears that a person is trying to cause a business to file a false or incomplete Form 8300.

- There is a sign of possible illegal activity.

Your business may report suspicious transactions by checking the "suspicious transaction" box (box 1b) on the top line of Form 8300. Businesses may also call the IRS Criminal Investigation Division Hotline at 800-800-2877, or the local IRS Criminal Investigation unit to report suspicious transactions. If a business suspects that a transaction is related to terrorist activity, the business should call the Financial Institutions Hotline at 866-556-3974.

Your business may voluntarily file a Form 8300 in those situations where the transaction is $10,000 or less but nevertheless suspicious. Because the Form 8300 is not required in those situations, there is no requirement to send a statement to the payer.

When to Report Payments

The amount of cash a customer uses for a transaction and when the customer makes the transaction are the determining factors for when the business must file Form 8300. Generally, a business must file Form 8300 within 15 days after they receive the cash. If the 15th day falls on a Saturday, a Sunday, or a holiday, the business must file the report on the next business day.

Multiple Payments

In some situations, the payer may arrange to pay in cash installments. If the first payment is more than $10,000, a business must file Form 8300 within 15 days. If the first payment is not more than $10,000, the business tracks the payments made within one year of the first payment. When the total cash payments exceed $10,000, the business must file Form 8300 within 15 days.

Recordkeeping

Your business should keep a copy of every Form 8300 it files, as well as the required statements it sends to its customers, for at least five years from the date filed.

Taxpayer Identification Number (TIN)

A business must obtain the correct TIN of the person(s) from whom they receive the cash.

Civil Penalties

The penalty for intentional disregard of the requirement to timely file a Form 8300 or to include all required, correct information is the greater of:

- $25,000

- The amount of cash received in the transaction, not to exceed $100,000.

The penalty applies to each failure.

Criminal Penalties

Any person who willfully files a Form 8300 that is false with regard to a material matter may be fined up to $100,000 ($500,000 in the case of a corporation), and/or imprisoned up to three years, plus the costs of prosecution.

Truth In Lending Act

Our next topic of discussion is the Truth In Lending Act and the Consumer Leasing Act.

Truth in Lending Act

This is a federal law enacted in 1968 with the intention of protecting consumers in their dealings with lenders and creditors. The Truth in Lending Act (TILA) was implemented by the Federal Reserve through a series of regulations.

Most of the specific requirements imposed by TILA are found in Regulation Z, so a reference to the requirements of TILA usually refers to the requirements contained in Regulation Z, as well as the statute itself.

Consumer Leasing Act

The Consumer Leasing Act (15 USC 1667 et seq) (CLA) was passed in 1976 to assure that meaningful and accurate disclosure of lease terms is provided to consumers before entering into a contract. It applies to consumer leases of personal property. With this information, consumers can more easily compare one lease with another, as well as compare the cost of leasing with the cost of buying on credit or the cost of paying cash.

In addition, the CLA puts limits on balloon payments, sometimes due at the end of a lease, and it also regulates advertising.

Originally, the CLA was part of the Truth in Lending Act and was implemented by Regulation Z. When Regulation Z was revised in 1981, Regulation M was issued and contained those provisions that govern consumer leases.

TILA Disclosures

A car dealership is required to provide TILA disclosures before the consumer has executed a Retail Installment Sales Contract. Virtually all RISC forms provided by the lenders contain TILA Disclosures; however, best practice is to provide a separate TILA disclosure statement.

Below are the necessary disclosures:

- The creditor's identity

- The amount financed, including a brief description of the term

- Itemization of the amount financed

- Finance charge

- The down payment and the total sales price

- APR

- Payment schedule, including the total number of payments, amounts, and timing of payments required to repay the loan

- A prepayment statement

- Charge that may be imposed prior to the maturity of the contract

- Exclusion of the cost of insurance from the finance charge & fees

- A statement that the consumer should refer to the appropriate contract document for the specifics of defaults, pre-payment penalties, default, etc.

CLA Disclosures

Your car dealership is required to provide CLA disclosures before the consumer has executed the Lease Agreement. Virtually all

Consumer Lease Agreements provided by lenders contain CLA disclosures; however, best practice is to provide a separate CLA disclosure statement.

Below are the necessary disclosures:

- Description of the leased property

- Amount due at lease signing or delivery, including other charges, taxes, fees, insurance, delinquency penalties and charges

- Payment schedule and total amount of periodic payments, including the total number of payments

- Payment calculation

- Rate limitation information

- Early-termination information

- Liability resulting from the residual value and net realizable value

- Maintenance responsibilities

- Option to purchase

- Statement referencing non-segregated disclosures

- Right of appraisal

- Liability at the end of the lease term, based on the residual value

- Warranties or guarantees

- Security interest

Truth in Lending and Consumer Leasing Act Penalties

Both the Truth in Lending Act and the Consumer Leasing Act Regulation Z and Regulation M carry serious penalties for willful and knowing violations. Maximum criminal liability for willful and knowing violation is a fine up to $5,000 and imprisonment of up to one year.

Fair Credit Compliance Program

Now let's talk about Fair Credit Compliance Program.

According to the National Association of Automobile Dealers, the Equal Credit Opportunity Act and its implementing Regulation B prohibits against discriminating against credit applicants on the basis of their race, color, religion, national origin, sex, marital status, age, and other factors.

Regulation B states that this prohibition does not just apply to intentional discrimination, but also to credit practices that appear neutral but nevertheless result in negative disparate impact on customers who are members of one of those protected classes.

Disparate impact can be discovered through statistical evaluation of past credit transactions. In order to comply with ECOA, it is not enough to train dealership employees to consider prohibited factors before making credit decisions. You need to implement a Fair Credit Policy. To avoid accusations of discrimination, dealerships must establish a means of compensation where the amount of finance income earned does not vary from customer to customer.

While you want to ensure that all customers are treated fairly, you also want to preserve sufficient flexibility to accommodate scenarios that may benefit customers, such as the "meet or beat" dynamic. One way to accomplish this is to establish a pre-set amount of compensation but allow for downward adjustments to that amount in the event that one or more pre-determined conditions occur.

Let's examine pre-determined allowable deviations:

- Dealer participation is limited by finance source—the lending source caps dealer mark-up

- Monthly payment constraint—rate mark-up may be reduced to meet customer's budget

- Competitive offer—rate mark-up may be reduced to meet or beat a competitive offer

- Dealership promotional financing offer—rate mark-up may be reduced to extend a promotional offer

- Manufacturer subvention program—customer qualifies for subvention program

- Dealership employee incentive offer—rate mark-up may be reduced to extend this offer

- Dealership inventory reduction—the Fair Credit Program must first define which vehicles qualify for the inventory reduction before the rate mark-up may be reduced

To establish an effective Fair Credit Program, you must:

- Develop a written policy

- Determine your pre-set mark-up rate

- Develop the inventory reduction criteria

- Create a Dealer Participation Certification Form

You will also need to appoint a fair-credit program coordinator, who is responsible for establishing a pre-set rate of dealer participation to be included in all credit offers that the dealership extends to customers. Furthermore, the program coordinator must outline pre-determined allowable deviations.

Any time an employee arranges a credit sale with a customer, he must complete, sign and date the Dealer Participation Certification form and then place the form in the deal jacket.

The program coordinator should review each credit sale within two business days of the sale to ensure that the employee who arranged the transaction properly executed a Dealer Participation Certification. The Program Coordinator may not have participated in the credit transaction under review.

If the program coordinator determines that the form was improperly filled out, the Coordinator notes the defect on the form and initiates appropriate corrective action. Such action includes:

- Ensuring that the customer receives a reduced interest rate or a refund if the transaction should have resulted in a lower interest rate for the customer

- Ensuring that appropriate corrective action is taken with the employee who improperly executed the form

If the reviewer is not the program coordinator, the reviewer should promptly notify the program coordinator of the defect. The program coordinator then coordinates with the general manager to ensure such corrective action was carried out. Upon completion of the review, the program coordinator completes, signs, and dates the Form's Reviewer Certification.

The program coordinator is also responsible for training new and existing employees on the procedures, and the training must be documented.

The program coordinator must submit a yearly report to the Board of Directors outlining your state of compliance and any recommendations.

Uniform F&I Product Pricing

F&I products is the next area of interest for both federal and state agencies. The idea here is pretty simple—white males generally pay less for F&I products than minorities do. In order to avoid getting into trouble, you should create a standard price list of all the F&I products you offer. For example, if you mark-up every service contract by $1000, then any deviation from that must be documented and the reason explained. Most reasons for the price deviation that we outlined before would work here as well.

Risk-Based Pricing

The Federal Trade Commission (FTC) began enforcement of the Risk-Based Pricing Rule on January 1st, 2011. This rule affects all car dealerships that pull credit reports on consumers, and failure to comply can result in heavy fines. Under the Risk-Based Pricing Rule, your dealership is required to present a notice to each consumer who has a credit report pulled. The notice must include their credit score, if they have one, and other information including key factors that may have adversely affected their score. Your finance managers must comply with this rule at all times.

Risk-Based Pricing is a great sales tool as well, as it shows the customer's credit score and how it compares to the rest of the population. Utlizing risk-based pricing disclosure in the sales process makes it easier to explain why the customer doesn't qualify for a particular interest rate or lease special. This type of third party validation is priceless.

Adverse Action Notice

Under the Fair Credit Reporting Act (FCRA) and the Equal Credit Opportunity Act (ECOA), adverse action is defined as "a denial or revocation of credit, a change in the terms of an existing credit arrangement, or a refusal to grant credit in substantially the amount or on substantially the terms requested." Therefore, any time a decision about a consumer's credit is made based entirely or in part on information contained in a credit report, your dealership is required to issue an Adverse Action notice. This applies to consumers in a number of different situations:

- If credit is denied

- If credit is not submitted for approval

- If credit is not granted with the terms requested

- If credit is accepted for an initial offer, but later rejected for a counteroffer

Even though the requirements seem straightforward, it isn't always easy to identify which consumers warrant an Adverse Action letter or how this fits into your sales process.

I strongly recommend that you contact Dealertrack or RouteOne and sign up for their Adverse Action Notice. For a nominal fee, they will mail out an Adverse Action Notice to your customers on your behalf.

Zero Tolerance Policies

Now let's discuss the major risks associated with day-to-day operations of a finance department. They are:

- Falsifying credit applications

- Power booking used cars

- Payment packing

- Jamming F&I products

I strongly recommend that you have a zero-tolerance policy for finance managers who engage in these practices.

Falsifying credit applications

Unscrupulous finance managers reduce rent expense, increase income, or pad years on the job in order to get a larger advance from the bank. It is extremely easy to falsify proof of income—just go to paystubb.com and for $7 you will have an ADP-formatted paystub in a matter of two minutes.

Power booking used cars

A finance manager might exaggerate the value of used car by telling the bank that it has options that it doesn't have, such as leather interior or a sunroof. Such a practice results in a larger advance from the bank.

Payment packing and jamming F&I products.

Payment packing happens after the finance manager has obtained approval from the bank. Payment packing is the deceptive act of presenting inflated monthly car loan payments to customers during negotiations. Jamming F&I products is slipping products into these inflated car payments without the customer's knowledge and consent.

The end result of such practices is high payments, cancellations, customer complaints, reputational damage, and repossessions.

These offenses are high on the agenda of state and federal law enforcement agencies. New York's Attorney General has gone after numerous car dealers in the last three years, collecting millions of dollars in fines and penalties. Recently, a Nissan dealership in New York was fined $298,000 and Hyundai dealership in New Jersey was fined $136,000 for engaging in these practices.

Consequences for the Dealer Principal

You should understand the risks of ignoring or overlooking such offences.

1. Reputational Damage. This is a big deal in the digital age, especially when customers can leave reviews in real-time—reviews that can lead to loss of market share. This is a slow death. Potential customers steer clear, as they take these reviews seriously. This is similar to your researching restaurants and avoiding 1-, 2-, and 3-star establishments.

2. Fines & Penalties. These can have dire financial consequences. New York Honda was fined $13 million for payment packing and jamming of F&I products. This happened to be one of the largest Honda dealerships in the country, and while they were able to sustain a financial hit of this magnitude, most dealerships are not in a position to write a $13 million check.

3. Civil & Criminal Charges. Again, this is bad for reputation and it's costly. In addition, it diverts the dealer's attention away from selling cars, parts, and labor.

4. Going out of business. This is the ultimate consequence of engaging in noncompliant practices. The collapse of Bill Heard Chevrolet, the 13th largest auto group at the time, is a perfect example.

Two Reasons For A Robust Compliance Program

Now let's put it all in perspective. There are two major reasons for maintaining a robust compliance program in F&I:

1. It helps you avoid paying hundreds of thousands or even millions of dollars in fines and penalties for non-compliant practices.

2. It makes the sales process more transparent, which is what today's consumer expects.

Ultimately your dealership saves money by avoiding fines, while making more money because transparent sales processes increase customer satisfaction and retention.

Remember, the name of the game is customer satisfaction and retention.

5
SERVICE

THE PARTS AND Service department is an amazing profit generator. However, many general managers and dealer principals do not understand this. This situation is easy to explain once you realize that a vast majority of general managers, dealer principals, and partners came up through sales. Only 3% come up through the fixed ops side of the business.

Fixed ops is not nuclear physics, and once you understand the foundation, you will begin to develop an appreciation for the back of the house. Understanding Parts and Service will not only help you make more money now, it will help you survive a sales downturn.

We will review the following topics:

- Service department marketing and advertising

- Service advisor workload and training

- Menu selling/one-line repair orders

- Utilizing technology in service

- Shop utilization and tech proficiency

- Critical KPI's

- Pickup and delivery

- Parts sales

- Parts personnel training

The best advice I can give you is this—if you are serious about understanding fixed ops, then you have to spend time in the service drive. Move your office from the showroom to the service department. Be in the trenches—that's the only way to learn.

Importance of Service and Parts

In order to be successful, you have to recognize that service and parts are as important as sales and F&I. A dealership will often treat its sales and F&I departments better, investing more money in their development, than fixed ops. This is especially true when it comes to allocating advertising and training dollars. When was the last time you bought lunch for your techs and service advisors? I bet you do it all the time for your salespeople and finance managers. When was the last time someone from fixed ops was an employee of the month?

Running a service department is not something you do to satisfy your franchise agreement. Your service department is where you print money. So let's start with the basics.

Google "oil change" and your dealership's zip code. I guarantee that every independent mechanic within that zip code will show up on the first page of Google. Does your dealership show up? If not, do you think this is a problem?

You should insist that your sales department show up on the first page of a Google search, and your advertising agency should be making that happen.

Service Department Advertising

Every general manager knows (or should know) how much his dealership spends on advertising per car sold. For example, if you spend $400 per car and plan on selling 100 cars per month, you will need to have a $40,000 monthly advertising budget.

One of the main reasons to advertise your service department is to increase service retention. The majority of your customers end up doing oil changes and preventive maintenance at national chains such as Jiffy Lube or independent mechanics. Service retention goes down by 80% once the factory warranty expires. That's because customers perceive national chains as convenient and less expensive.

In reality, prices charged by dealerships are the same and sometimes even less. Your advertising campaign must address the fact that it is convenient and cost effective to use your service department. Ultimately, if you treat customers well during the warranty period, then they will stay with you.

When it comes to a service department's advertising dollars, most dealerships allocate some small arbitrary amount that pays for an EOM mailer.

Start with the basics. What are the most common service-related searches? Once you know what these are, make sure that your service department shows up either via Search Engine Optimization (that means that you will need dedicated web pages on your site for each search) and via Pay-Per-Click advertising (that means that you are bidding on certain key words).

Below are the top 8 most frequent searches. Try every one of them and see if your dealership shows up on the first page. If you are not on the first page, then frankly you do not exist.

Top 8 Most Common Vehicle Repairs

- Oil/oil filter change

- Wiper blades replacement

- Replace air filter

- Scheduled maintenance

- New tires

- Battery replacement

- Brake work

- Antifreeze added

There are other types of advertising to consider. Are you actively marketing to out-of-warranty vehicle owners in your area? The average age of a car is 11.5 years, so there are plenty of cars to go after. You can find these cars in your customer database and/or buy a list of registrations from a list broker.

Remember, your service department doesn't exist in a vacuum; it is attached to a sales department. Salespeople **must**—and I can't stress this enough—introduce each buyer to the service department. Your customers deserve to know that you have state-of-the-art equipment and factory-trained techs who work on very sophisticated vehicles.

Your customers must know that you've invested a ton of money into the customer waiting area (furniture, computers, WIFI, TV, etc.) should they choose to wait. They also need to know that you offer loaners, rideshare, and pickup and delivery. Note that pickup and delivery will become more popular because of COVID-19.

What about results? It's crucial that you develop a formula for tracking the success of your marketing and advertising. Start small—$20 per repair order—and see where it takes you.

Vendors

Fixed Ops Digital. www.fixedopsdigital.com

Service department marketing and advertising is all they do. They provide the following:

- Dealer Wallet

- Service Menu Page

- Drive Service SEO

And so much more.

Service Advisor Workload and Training

Do you know how much time a service advisor needs to spend with a customer? No need to guess. Just go to the service drive with a stopwatch and figure it out. Between greeting, active walk-around, write-up, pulling vehicle history, going through menu presentation, making recommendations, and active delivery, it is fair to allocate 30 minutes per customer. That's two customers per hour. Let's allocate another two hours to communicating with techs, the parts department, customers, and doing paperwork. Make sure that the number of technicians per service advisor is between 4 and 5.

If your service advisors are seeing more than 12 customers per day, then they are leaving money on the table. Why? Because they don't have enough time to properly do their job. If this case, they are no longer service advisors; they are order takers. And order takers do not make money. This is similar to finance managers taking more than 80 turns per month. At that point, they are just billers.

Now that we figured out proper workload, we need to make sure that the service advisors have adequate sales training to get the job done. Training is a given in the sales department. When I was a general manager, I trained my salespeople every Saturday. In addition, they had product knowledge and phone skills training on a monthly basis.

How many general managers are actively participating in the sales training of service advisors? My guess is no more than 3%. Here is another question: how many service managers are conducting sales training on a weekly basis?

Most dealerships have monthly bonuses for salespeople (volume bonus, highest gross profit bonus). In addition, there are Saturday bonuses (first spot, most cars sold, highest gross). Do you have anything remotely similar for your service advisors? In most cases, the answer is no. Below are a few bonus examples that apply to service:

- Most wheel alignments sold

- Most labor hours sold

- Most preventive maintenance sold

Sales training for service advisors is not that much different from the training that salespeople receive. It starts with proper dress code and the ability to meet and greet and build rapport.

In order to accomplish this, you need to view your service manager as a sales manager. This paradigm shift will have you laughing all the way to the bank.

It is up to you to make sure that your service director is on the same page with you. Below are the non-negotiables that I recommend you incorporate into your training.

1. **Answer the phone quickly and politely.** The key word here is "answer." I can't tell how many times service-department customers are sent to voicemail or into a black hole. In comparison, independent mechanics have no problem answering phones.

2. **Greet customers in the service drive.** Customers pulling into the service drive must have their presence acknowledged right away (5 seconds or less), and advisors must be smiling and friendly.

3. **Provide point-of-sale marketing materials.** Provide these materials for customers to review while they are pulling up to meet the advisor. Examples include a detail menu, accessories, and new car specials. Remember: most customers do not know what you have to offer.

4. **Build rapport.** The advisor must approach the customer (not the other way around) and greet the customer by name. Ask questions and **listen** to the answers.

Here are some other suggestions for your service department.

✓ **Perform a walk-around with each and every customer**. It is important to involve the customer in the walk-around in order to increase the chance of a sale: for example, tires, dent repair, and windshield wiper replacement. Don't forget to touch scratches and dents, open the hood and check the fluids, and check tire pressure. Consider using Hunter equipment to measure tire thread and wheel alignment.

Like showroom walk-arounds, this is something your advisors need to practice. Have your advisors compete, taking turns role-playing. And offer bonuses for those who excel.

✓ **Fill out an inspection sheet.** Introduce an inspection sheet right away so that the customer aren't caught by surprise with additional work.

✓ **Inspect the vehicle within 30 minutes of being racked.** Time is money, and turnaround time matters. Whip out your stopwatch and go see how long it takes in your service employees to complete an inspection.

✓ **Follow-up with customers.** Your advisors must be able to contact the customer for an authorization to do the work. I can't stress this enough—you must use technology that allows your employees to text/email customers. You must use technology that allows you to send videos—seeing is believing, and this will help you increase your closing ratio. Also, you must use technology that allows you to process payments. The proper use of technology will reduce friction for both service advisors/techs and for customers.

✓ **Record declined services.** Decline services must be recorded on the repair order. The best sales training and technology doesn't guarantee a 100% closing ratio. Make sure your advisors record declined services on the repair order for future follow-up. (Keep in mind that decline lines indicate that the advisors are in fact offering the work, even if it's declined.) Target a 30% closing ratio on declined services follow-up. Make sure your advisors are following up within 30-45 days.

✓ **Track one-line item repair orders.** If your one-line item repair orders exceed 30%, it's a sign of either:

- Advisor work overload

- Lack of training

- Poor salesmanship

✓ **Be ready for each appointment.** If the customer made an appointment, make sure to pull vehicle service history and know everything about their car.

✓ **Discuss a CSI.** Yes, I said it. CSI (Customer Satisfaction Index) is not a dirty secret. Tell your customers you will provide an amazing service and when they receive a survey in the mail they must answer it accordingly. The key here is to make sure that your advisors are truly committed to providing an incredible service.

✓ **Use active delivery.** When you require your service advisors to actively deliver cars, they will make sure that the cars are perfect and that all customer concerns are addressed. Service advisors are your last line of defense.

✓ **Under promise and over-deliver.** This is an art, not science. Provide a free car wash, offer a discount even if the customer didn't ask for it, give a coupon for the next visit. Be creative and exceed the customer's expectations.

It's critical that you hold service advisors accountable. Set expectations for hours-per-repair order on customer paid labor. Figure out what the 12-month average is and set your expectations a little lower. Then raise it every 90 days. Make sure that you set goals that are achievable and realistic. This is exactly what you do in sales and F&I—you hold salespeople accountable and expect them to make a certain amount of appointments and sales. Same goes for finance managers. Why shouldn't you expect the same accountability from your service advisors?

Vendors

Chris Collins. www.chriscollins.com

Chris Collins provides online training for service personnel. Learn how to:

- Build menus that convert

- Increase your ELR by $15-$25 by using new pricing strategies

- Implement inspection systems that self-manage

- Read and comprehend financial statements

- Improve your leadership skills

- Create effective shop loading and dispatching systems

- Effectively hire and recruit top talent

- Become a master of time management (i.e. work/life balance)

- And much, much more including hours of OnDemand online coursework

Using Technology in the Service Department

Could you do a deal without Dealertrack/RouteOne and Dealer Management Software (DMS)? Probably. But it would be time consuming and inefficient. The same goes for your service department. Using state-of-the-art technology will help you book more appointments, improve dispatch, and upsell additional work.

Don't fight technology; embrace it. During COVID-19, many dealers were open for service only, and it was absolutely mind-blowing to see how many of them didn't have an online appointment scheduler on their websites.

Vendor

Update Promise. www.updatepromise.com
Update Promise automates communication between service departments and service customers. In addition, customers can pay for repairs right from their phone.

XTIME. www.xtime.com
They offer a full spectrum of service drive applications:

- Invite

- Schedule

- Engage

- Inspect

Critical KPIs to Monitor in Service

You can't manage what you can't measure. Most general managers and dealer principals know what to expect in sales and F&I. They know, or at least have an idea of, the number of incoming leads, appointment ratio, show ratio, closing ratio, product penetration percentage, and overall PVR. But what about the service department?

Production Capacity

Before we go into service KPIs, we need to figure out your shop's production capacity. Let's calculate your daily hours. To do this, multiply the number of technicians you have by the number of production hours per technician per day. That total is the number of hours you could be producing in a day. For example, if you have ten techs who work an 8-hour shift, then you should be producing a minimum of 80 hours per day. If you are open for a double shift, then expect to produce 160 hours per day.

Knowing this number will make everything else much clearer and will help you set benchmarks.

Keep in mind that due to COVID-19, more customers will be interested in pickup and delivery, and that means you must start getting ready to be open 24 hours a day.

Shop efficiency. At the very minimum, your goal should be 100% efficiency; meaning your shop capacity equals shop efficiency. Using the previous example: if your shop is billing exactly 80 hours per day, then you are at 100% efficiency. The good news is, you can be at 110%, 120%, and even 150% efficiency. For example, if your techs bill 96 hours, you are 120% efficiency, and if they bill 120 hours, your shop is at 150% efficiency. How do you accomplish a high level of efficiency? Below are five factors that determine efficiency.

1. **Tech training.** Cars are becoming computers on wheels, and it seems that technology is evolving on a daily basis. Make sure that your techs are up-to-date on all OEM training. Hold them accountable!

2. **Proper dispatching.** Jobs cannot be randomly assigned. Make sure there is a match between the job and the tech's expertise.

3. **Timely job assignment.** Repair orders must not be sitting on the advisor's or service manager's desk for no reason.

4. **Properly filled out repair orders.** Service writers must clearly communicate the customer's concern so that techs do not waste any time.

5. **Parts availability.** Efficiency depends on parts being in stock. If parts are not in stock, they must be ordered right away.

Now that you understand shop capacity and shop efficiency, the first thing you will need to monitor is how many hours your shop produces on a daily basis. And that's how you know if you are on track to hit your daily/weekly/monthly goal. Using our example, if your shop produced 60 hours instead of an expected 80 hours, you need to identify the problem and fix it right away.

Hours Sold Per Repair Order

Although the ideal number of hours per repair order depends on the franchise, it safe to say that everyone would like to be at 2.5 hours per repair order. How do you get there? First, your techs must perform a Multipoint Vehicle Inspection on each vehicle, and it had better be attached to the repair order. Better yet, attach pictures to the multipoint inspection. Second, your advisors must be able to sell additional work.

Effective Labor Rate

In the perfect world, your effective labor rate would be equal to or greater than your posted labor rate. Unfortunately, in most cases it is not. To calculate effective labor rate (ELR), divide the total labor sales (in dollars) for the month by total number of labor hours. You must know your effective labor rate; it's as important as knowing your PVR. Why would the effective labor rate be lower than your posted labor rate? There are several reasons. First, oil changes and other competitive items designed to bring customers in will lower ELR. Second, discounting by service advisors will negatively impact ELR. Third, improper job pricing and dispatching result in lower ELR. Training service advisors, dispatchers, and techs, and focusing on preventive maintenance sales will help you raise your effective labor rate.

Shop Policy Expense

The goal of every service department should be: Fix it right the first time. For a variety of reasons, it is not always possible to get it right the first time, and your shop will have to absorb the costs associated with making it right for the customer.

There are two schools of thought when it comes to shop policy. First, that shop policy expense shouldn't exceed 1% of total labor sales. Second (and it's the one I prefer), that a fixed dollar amount should be allocated each month to each service advisor to do the right thing. For example, there are service departments that allow $1500 per advisor, per month, while others allow for unlimited dollar amounts. This doesn't mean that the service advisors actually max out their policy allowance; it simply means that they have the tools at their disposal to do the right thing. And you will always lose in the court of public opinion if you don't do the right thing.

Warranty Compliance

A big chunk of service revenue comes from doing warranty work. It is your responsibility to properly diagnose, document, and fix a vehicle under warranty. If the warranty work is not properly submitted, the manufacturer has the legal right to charge back. You have two options when it comes to warranty compliance—either have an in-house warranty administrator or hire a third-party. Either approach is fine as long as you are on top of warranty compliance. The last thing you want to do is to record a profit on the financial statement, and then get charged back. Make sure that tech notes are clear. Moreover, I encourage you to scan repair orders, because it will be much easier to locate them in case of an OEM warranty audit.

Service Absorption

Absorption is calculated by dividing total fixed gross profit (parts, service, collision) by total fixed expenses for the dealership. The higher the number, the better. Some dealers can never get to 100%, while others are at 120%. Figure out where you stand today and set a goal of increasing service absorption. High service absorption should help you increase new/used car sales and grab market share because you will be able to offer a more competitive price.

Increasing Effective Labor Rate

Once you know your effective labor rate, you can start working on its improvement. What can you do to accomplish this?

Sell preventive maintenance. Create a menu that lists different preventive maintenance options for different mileage bands. Require service advisors to present the menu to all customers. We are all familiar with the 300% rule in F&I— Present 100% of products to 100% of customers 100% of the time. Use the same approach in your service department.

Display this menu on your website, have a printed version by each advisor and also in the customer waiting area. Make sure that your menu includes brakes and tires. Set a goal of 50% penetration.

Monitor one-line item repair orders. As discussed above, you absolutely have to track these numbers. Let service advisors know that you are not willing to tolerate anything above 30%.

Attract out-of-warranty vehicles. Develop a marketing campaign to attract out-of-warranty vehicles. Determine the number of units in operation in your area and actively go after these cars.

Maintain internal labor rate. Do not discount your internal labor rate. In other words, your used car department pays the same rate as any customer. This is not something that is open for negotiation.

Monitor discounting. Repair-order discounts must be approved and signed by the service manager. Do not allow service advisors to discount on their own!

Train. Train. Train. It is your responsibility as the leader to provide the necessary training for your staff to succeed. Sales training for service advisors is a must and has to be done on a regular basis. Training is something you do, not something you did.

Vendors

Larry Edwards and Associates. www.larryedwardsassociates.com

Larry Edwards is a dedicated fixed ops professional. His vast experience will help you fine-tune your service/parts/collision shop.

M5 Management Services. www.m5ms.com

We help Dealership, OEM, and Corporate clients improve their fixed operations business in the parts, service, and collision centers. We have extensive experience in every area of fixed operations management. Our core strength is our ability to offer our clients proven techniques and concepts that work.

Pickup And Home Delivery

Prior to the COVID-19 pandemic, most dealers (and I mean more than 95%) would not offer pickup and delivery to their service customers. Why? It's the same reason they didn't take advantage of digital retail in their sales and F&I departments: people are afraid of change. And car dealers are no different.

Post COVID-19 reality is different and requires a tectonic shift in dealership operations. Customers are no longer interested in coming in and waiting for their car to be worked on. If you can't provide pickup and delivery or mobile service, your customers will find someone who can. The choice is yours—either reduce friction and make it easy and convenient for your customers to get their cars serviced with you, or watch your customer base slowly disappear.

Once you figure out the logistics, you will find that your dollars-per-repair-order are going to double and your repair order count will triple. That's because customers are much more willing to approve additional work from the comfort of their home. Eventually you will be open 24 hours per day and your shop utilization will be 100%.

Stop making excuses and jump in. You will thank me later when you are laughing all the way to the bank.

Vendors

RedCap. www.getredcap.com
Easily offer a modern consumer experience that compliments your brands objectives. Our compete turn-key program is tailored to work within your service drive's process, delivers an experience to your customers that you design, and is proven to scale across your customer base.

Shop Safety

We spend a lot of time on F&I compliance because F&I can be a source of fines and penalties. The same goes for your service department. The Occupational Safety and Health Administration (OSHA) is tasked with ensuring safe and healthy working conditions for working men and women. OSHA violations are expensive and a pain to deal with.

Instilling a safety mindset in your shop is important, and the first step is training. Safety training must be mandatory and ongoing. There are three reasons for safety training. First, it is good for employee morale—technicians see that the organization cares about their well-being. Second, it reduces liability associated with OSHA violations. Third, and most importantly, safety training prevents injuries.

Let's monetize the cost of an injury to a technician. He produces 40 hours per week at $125 per hour. That's $5000 in gross labor sales. Generally speaking, there is a 1:1 ratio between labor and parts sales, so that's another $5000 in gross parts sales. An injury that results in a two-week absence means that the dealership will miss out on $20,000 in gross labor and parts sales.

So what are the elements of a comprehensive safety compliance program in the service department?

1. Hire a third party to conduct an audit in order to know where you stand.

2. Appoint a compliance officer and empower that officer to enforce your corporate policies and procedures.

3. Provide effective onboarding for new hires. Every new technician must complete all required safety training before being allowed to start working. The best way to deliver this training is through a cloud-based learning management system that allows techs to use any device anywhere and provides electronic paper trail.

4. Provide ongoing safety training for existing employees. Make sure that this training is documented; otherwise, it never happened.

5. Review and modify your health and safety program as new information and threats develop.

Make sure that your dealership service department provides the following safety training:

- Accident Causes, Prevention, and Control

- Back Safety

- Electrical Safety

- Hazardous Communications

- Personal Protective Equipment

- Bloodborne Pathogen Program

- Fire Safety

- First Aid

Prior to COVID-19, discussions about Personal Protective Equipment (PPE) were limited to goggles, ear plugs, protective gloves, nonslip footwear, etc. Now PPE means gloves, masks, Plexiglas dividers, and hand sanitizer. Make sure you have adequate supplies, written protocols for social distancing and sanitizing cars, and that you conduct regular, documented training.

6
PARTS

LET'S BE HONEST—IT is almost impossible to make money selling new cars. New car margins are nonexistent; however, most general managers and dealer principals obsess about it. Meanwhile, a parts department that can easily generate a 40%-50% gross profit is being treated like a stepchild. What other business has margins like this?

I can't recall ever seeing a dealer principal or a general manager in the parts department. Sometimes I think they don't even know where it is located. Think about it—the parts business is incredible.

- Your shop is your best customer.

- Body shops need you.

- The do-it-yourself community wants to buy from you.

- Digital retail allows you to sell across 50 states.

As I stated before, since most dealers and general managers come up through sales, they lack the appreciation for and understanding of parts sales. Once you understand that your parts department can be a source of steady income, you will begin investing in training, inventory, and advertising.

Answering the Phone

Let's start with the basics—answering the phone. What would you do if your salespeople answered the phone by saying "Sales, please hold"? We all know the answer—heads would roll. Unfortunately, this is an acceptable practice in the parts department, and ultimately the fault is yours.

It is a standard operating procedure to listen to incoming sales calls in the sales department. BDC managers, sales managers, general managers, and dealer principals do it all the time. They hire trainers, record calls, and buy CRM software to improve phone and follow-up skills. For some reason, however, most general managers and dealer principals cannot connect the dots and do the same for their parts department.

We all know how hard it is to get salespeople to say the right thing on the phone. It is no different for parts personnel. Before setting any goals or looking at KPI's, you need to teach your parts department staff how to answer the phone properly and how to follow-up with existing and potential customers.

Fortunately, you don't need to hire a trainer; this is something you can do yourself. You have enough sales training to know the basics:

1. Don't put people on hold.

2. Introduce yourself.

3. Ask for customer's contact information and enter it into the CRM. (How many of you even have a CRM in parts?)

4. Build value instead of discounting.

5. Follow-up if they don't buy.

6. Follow-up if they do buy.

7. Provide the best service possible.

Now more than ever phone skills and online sales will make or break you. There are no shortcuts—you need to get involved; there is no other way.

Ultimately, it is your responsibility to make sure that your parts manager understands that he or she is in business of **selling** parts.

Buying Parts

As a new car dealer, you buy parts from your OEM. Your franchise agreement allows you to turn around and sell these OEM parts to the consumer. This gives you the opportunity to make a healthy profit margin.

What if I told you that you can make money twice—first when you buy parts, and second when you sell them? Once you purchase enough to satisfy your OEM, start looking elsewhere. Your OEM is not your only supply source. Nothing is stopping you from buying parts from another dealer. You can often purchase parts 30 cents on the dollar, especially now, when many dealers will have to close doors due to COVID-19.

Your parts manager is no different from your used car buyer. They are both tasked with getting you the best available inventory for the least amount of money. This might seem like common sense to you, but remember that common sense is not that common. Make sure that you have job descriptions in writing for all positions and especially for parts personnel.

Besides purchasing parts (from your OEM or independent suppliers), your parts manager also buys chemicals, oil, and accessories. Make sure you do a periodic vendor review, because kickbacks are common, and you want to make sure that you are getting the best deal possible.

Parts Gross Profit

Selling parts is not like selling cars—you actually make money doing it! Your best customer is your shop, so make sure that you charge your shop the same rate as any other retail customer—45% gross profit is what you are looking for. This is no different from charging your used car department the customer pay labor rate.

Your parts counter must produce the same 45% gross profit. Make sure that your DMS price guide is set accordingly. Discounting must be approved by the parts manager. Run a price override report daily to keep your finger on the pulse.

Wholesale Parts Sales

Wholesale is not for everybody. Profit margins are significantly lower and there are additional costs to consider—parts delivery personnel, delivery vehicles, additional capital allocated to parts inventory, bad debt, and accounting costs just to name a few.

It all comes down to one thing: are you capable of managing it? Wholesale is no different from retail in that you have advertise, manage customer relationships, collect, and ultimately provide awesome customer service. If you want to succeed in wholesale, you must fully commit to running a wholesale parts business.

The car business is a people business, and that means personal relationships matter greatly. Make sure your parts manager visits local body and repair shops to establish a relationship. Make sure it is easy for your regular customers to do business with you.

The internet is here to stay, and digital retail isn't something you should do only in your personal life. Digital retail means that you have an e-commerce tool for your wholesale customers. It is all about removing friction.

Parts obsolescence is a real issue and must be managed at all times. Run reports to make sure that you don't overstock certain parts. Keep in mind that you might be able to sell these parts to other stores in your auto group. Moreover, eBay and Amazon are great avenues for selling your aging inventory at a discount.

Selling Parts Online

You have to crawl before you walk, and you have to walk before you run. This logic applies to selling online. Going from traditional face-to-face showroom interaction to selling cars online is not hard. It's **extremely hard**!

The best way to learn digital retail is via online parts sales. There is no title, registration, and there is no financing. Selling parts is as straightforward as it gets. The good news is, you are no longer limited to your local market. The whole country, and in some instances the whole world, is your market. You will need to figure out your advertising, pick the best digital retail tool that fits your needs, develop a fulfillment and shipping protocol, and design return procedures.

This undertaking requires you to fully commit, which means appointing a person whose sole responsibility is to figure out online parts sales. There are certain things to consider.

1. Will you selling from your dealership website or will you have a dedicated website for parts (for example, xyzchevyparts.com)?

2. Will you be selling on eBay, Amazon, or any other online marketplace?

3. Do you want to be an Amazon Prime seller?

4. What about a pricing strategy? I suggest you shop your competition and pricing accordingly.

5. You will need protocols in place that ensure good online reviews. You are dead on arrival if you are not going after online reviews.

Selling parts online will not only help you master digital retail, it will help you develop an additional source of revenue and ultimately help you survive during a sales downturn. We all know that when people delay a car purchase, they spend more on service and parts.

Vendors

Revolution Parts. www.revolutionparts.com

Great tool that will help you launch your parts and accessories online store. Will help you sell on eBay and Amazon in addition to your own store. Literally a one-stop shop for all your online parts sales needs.

Selling Accessories

Accessories are parts, and it is in your best interest to sell as many accessories as possible. Most dealers do not pay enough attention to accessories sales. Your parts manager must work together with the sales and finance department in order to create a culture that sells accessories.

According to Automotive News, 6 million new cars are accessorized in the first two years of ownership. Typical spending is between $300$800 per car and $1500 per truck. Here are the alarming statistics—only 5% of customers buy accessories from the dealership where they purchased their vehicle. There is a huge opportunity for you.

First and foremost, accessorize cars in the showroom. Instead of complaining about thin margins, make your inventory stand out from the competition; this will increase your profits. Accessorize, have an addendum sticker, and sell from strength. Create packages that finance managers can sell and make sure that you have these accessories in stock.

If you have room, put an accessorized car in the service waiting area. Let your service customers know what is available and make sure that you display prices that include installation for all of the accessories.

Do not keep your accessory business a secret. Promote it on your website, post videos of accessorized cars on your YouTube channel, join a local car club, conduct clinics, etc.

Below is a list of the most popular accessories by sales volume. Make sure you have these in stock and market them accordingly.

- Floor mats

- Window tinting

- Splash guards

- Alarms, vehicle recovery systems, etc.

- Body side moldings
- Step bars
- Cargo nets
- Wheel accessories
- Trailer hitches

Parts Obsolescence

Parts are similar to used cars—both are perishable items. Both will negatively impact your profits if you don't pay attention. Most of us are familiar with aging units when it comes to used-car inventory. We know that we need to track it and act accordingly.

Your parts manager must understand that one of his most important job duties is to reduce obsolescence. You can't eliminate it completely, but you can take steps to reduce it.

Run a report to make sure that parts obsolescence over 6 months doesn't exceed 25% of the inventory and that parts obsolescence over 12 months doesn't exceed 10% of inventory.

Take advantage of return programs and have clearly defined special-order programs. In other words, require prepayment for each and every special-order part. No exceptions.

Design smart return policies for both wholesale and retail customers. For example, require a 25% restocking fee on special-order parts.

Effectively dealing with parts obsolescence will help you free up capital that you can invest into parts that actually sell. The more times you turn your parts inventory, the more money you will make.

Quick Lube And Upselling

Quick lube must be a profitable business—otherwise Jiffy Lube, Valvoline, Firestone, and many others wouldn't exist. If you don't offer quick lube to your customers, then you are sending them to your competitors.

The quick-lube business is based on the concept of upsell, so your parts manager must be actively involved in monitoring upsell percentages of the following parts:

- Air filters

- Wiper blades

- Light bulbs

- Belts

- Cabin filters

- Batteries

- Transmission fluid flush

- Coolant change

- Tires

Set upsell goals and hold your quick lube advisors/techs accountable. This is similar to holding finance managers accountable for a certain product penetration. Make sure you have a motivational pay plan in place.

Time is money, and an oil change that takes longer than 30 minutes will feel like an eternity to your customers; it's likely they won't come back. One way to speed up the process is to create parts kits for express services and all maintenance work. Another way is to keep fast-moving parts in the techs' stalls. In addition, provide techs with walkie-talkies so that they can call in their parts and have them delivered to their stalls.

Parts Level Of Service

This is a very important metric that allows you to know what percentage of orders are filled off the shelf. Aim for a fill rate of 85%. If the number is higher than 85%, this means that your parts personnel are not recording lost sales in the DMS.

It's human nature to choose the path of least resistance, and a lot of parts-counter employees will not record a lost sale unless they absolutely have to. It is your responsibility to monitor this KPI and to make sure that all lost sales are recorded.

Days' Supply

Understanding days' supply will help allocate your capital better. You are better off investing into fast-moving parts rather than slow-moving parts. If money were free and parts obsolescence did not exist, then you would want to have every part number known to man in stock. Unfortunately, the real world doesn't work like that. You must use your capital wisely.

Eventually you will figure out the formula that works for your store. For now, start with the following KPI's:

- Maintenance parts—90 day supply

- Repair parts—30 day supply

- Body parts—10 day supply

Emergency Purchases

If you want to provide a high level of customer service, you will have to deal with emergency purchases. However, you must have your finger on the pulse when it comes to this metric because your profitability will be greatly impacted otherwise.

Emergency purchasing is the purchasing of parts from other dealers in your area for a low markup over cost. Sounds pretty innocent, right? It isn't. Once you account for administrative and pickup/delivery costs, time and productivity lost, you will realize that your net profit is evaporating right in front of your eyes.

Make sure to run a report in your DMS to verify that your emergency purchases do not exceed 3% of total purchases.

Perpetual Parts Inventory

There are two reasons why you need to audit your parts inventory.

1. To detect and prevent (if necessary) theft
2. To maximize the level of service or fill rate in order to optimize return on investment

Parts inventory is a never-ending process. Daily inventory is a must, and you should cycle through your inventory at least two times per year.

In addition, you should hire a third party to conduct a parts inventory audit once a year. It makes a huge difference when your parts personnel understand that you're paying attention.

DMS Settings and Tech Proficiency

Proper DMS settings are critical to a well-run parts department. Your DMS can be your best friend or your worst enemy. Most DMS systems are not intuitive, so you will need to call tech support and spend a considerable amount of time tweaking the settings. Your DMS must be programmed to:

- Increase parts availability

- Increase parts coverage

- Decrease emergency & special orders

- Decrease lost sales

- Increase purchase efficiency

- Increase fill-of-the-shelf rate

Optimizing these settings will help you sell more parts.

Equally important is the proficiency of your technicians. Tech proficiency means having the necessary technical knowledge and skills to diagnose and fix cars. It is in everybody's interest (dealer principal, general manager, service manager, and parts manager) to ensure that all techs are properly trained and participate in continuous education programs.

CONCLUSION

This is my fourth book on the auto industry, and I have written it because this business is complicated, sophisticated, and ever-changing. Automotive retail is changing slowly, and one of the main reasons for that are the franchise laws. I want to urge you to operate as though franchise laws don't exist to protect you. Carvana is not going anywhere and neither is Amazon. At some point they will join forces. Also, OEM's such as Tesla, Rivian, and many more are going to go directly to the consumer, bypassing the dealer network altogether.

At the end of the day, awesome customer service, whether in sales, service, or parts, will keep your customers coming back for more. Poor service and a cumbersome sales experience will drive them elsewhere—Carvana, CarMax, Tesla, Jiffy Lube, Firestone, Good Year, Valvoline, NAPA Parts, Pep Boys, etc.

COVID-19 is already having a profound effect on consumer behavior and the way in which we buy and service cars. I predict that there will be two types of dealers after this pandemic abates—the first will change their business operations, adopting frictionless digital and showroom retail; the second will hope that things go back to normal and that nothing needs to change. Unfortunately, the second type of dealer will be out of business. It is ultimately your choice whether to accept change. Consumers will continue to purchase cars. The only question is: Will they will be buying from you?

THANK YOU FOR READING!

PLEASE REACH OUT IF YOU HAVE ANY QUESTIONS, NEED HELP, OR JUST WANT TO TALK ABOUT CAR BUSINESS.

max@maxzanan.com
917-903-0312

Made in the USA
Las Vegas, NV
29 December 2020

14955317R00089